Meetings with Clients

A Self-Study Manual for a Builder's Frontline Personnel

Carol Smith

National Association of Home Builders
1201 15th Street, NW
Washington, DC 20005-2800
www.BuilderBooks.com

Meeting with Clients: A Self Study Manual for a Builder's Front-Line Personnel by Carol Smith

Christine B. Charlip	Publisher, BuilderBooks
Doris M. Tennyson	Senior Editor
Torrie Singletary	Production Editor
Circle Graphics	Composition
Midland	Printing
Gerald Howard	NAHB Executive Vice President and CEO
Mark Pursell	NAHB Senior Staff Vice President, Marketing & Sales Group
Lakisha Campbell	NAHB Staff Vice President, Publications Affinity Program

Printed in the United States.
10 09 08 07 06 1 2 3 4 5
ISBN 0-86718-526-0

Cataloging-in-Publication data available from the Library of Congress.

For further information, please contact:

BuilderBooks.com NAHB — A Service of National Association of Home Builders

National Association of Home Builders
1201 15th Street, NW
Washington, DC 20005-2800
800-223-2665
Visit us online at www.BuilderBooks.com

Contents

List of Figures viii

Carol Smith's Customer
Relations Series ix

About the Author and
Series Editor x

Acknowledgments xi

Introduction 1
How to Use this Guide
Raw Material 1
Client Meetings 2
   Policies and Procedures 2
   Predictable Situations 3
Terminology 3
Diskette 3

PART 1
Knowledge Is Power 5
The Raw Material of Service

1 Community 7

2 Company 9
Sales Presentation 9
Contract Session: Purchase
Agreement 11
Mortgage Application 11
Selections 13
Preconstruction Conference 13
Frame Stage Tour 14

Home Buyer Orientation 14
Closing 15
Warranty Service 15
Company Meetings and Reports 16

3 Home Construction 17

4 Product Profile 19
Standard House 19
   Changes in Production: Substitut-
   ing "Equal or Better" 19
   Slight Variations 20
Options and Upgrades 20
Custom Changes 20
Handouts and Displays 20

5 Maintenance and Warranty 22
Building Codes 22
Manufacturer's and Supplier's
Literature 23
Homeowner Manual 23
Builder Limited Warranty 23
Trade Shows, Conferences, and
Seminars 23

PART 2
The Meetings 27
*Common Elements and
Uncommon Skills*

6 Policies and Procedures 29
Schedule 29

Prepare **30**
 Predictions Versus Facts **30**
 Price and Experience **30**
  First-Time Buyers **30**
  Experienced Buyers **31**
  Victims of Negative
  Experience **31**
 Product Familiarity **31**
 Paperwork **31**
 Conduct **32**
Follow Through **32**

**7 Attitudes, Communication Skills,
and Habits That Help 33**
Accountability **33**
Body Language **33**
 Eye Contact **34**
 Smiling **34**
 Gestures **34**
 Posture **34**
 Tone of Voice **35**
Judgment Calls **35**
 Physical Judgment: The Documents
 and the House **35**
 Circumstantial Judgment: The
 Client's Side of the Story **35**
  Objectivity **35**
  Listening **35**
  Research **35**
  Common Sense **36**
 Image Judgment: Reputation at
 Risk **36**
  Low Survey Scores **36**
  Negative Word-of-Mouth **36**
  Going Over Your Head **36**
  Revenge Lists **36**
  Complaints to Sales **36**
  Instigating **36**
  Drama **36**
  Media **36**
  Consumer Protection Entities **36**
  Arbitration **37**
  Litigation **37**
  Precedent **37**
  Budget **37**
  Complaints **37**

 Delays **37**
 Self-Esteem **37**
Listening **37**
Saying No **38**
 Soft No **38**
 Terminal No **38**
Service Maturity **38**
When Things Go Wrong **39**

8 Predictable Situations 41
Abusive Clients **41**
Baiting **41**
Buyers Disagree with Each Other **42**
Buyers Misquote or Misunderstand **42**
Dishonest Client **42**
Emergencies **43**
Gender Bias **43**
Going Over Your Head **44**
Good Cop, Bad Cop **44**
Home Improvement Store
Syndrome **45**
I'll Be Glad to Find Out **45**
Interruptions: Phones, Pagers, or
People **46**
Inventory Sale **46**
Language Barriers **46**
Left-Out Spouse **47**
 Physical **47**
 Emotional **47**
 Communication **47**
Let's Make a Deal **48**
Out-of-State Buyers **48**
Personality Conflict **48**
Scheduling Issues **48**
 Buyers Are Late **49**
 Buyers Are Unavailable **49**
 Buyers Insist on Off-Hours
 Appointments **49**
Silence Is Golden **49**
Television and the Internet **50**
Third Parties **50**
 Real Estate Agent **51**
 Private Home Inspector **51**
Unrealistic Expectations **52**
What If . . . ? **52**
Won't Take No for an Answer **52**

PART 3 Preconstruction Conference 53
Expectations for the Building Process

Transfer of Trust 53
Confirmation of Plans and
    Specifications 53
Unresolved Issues 54
Preparation Check and Balance 54
Attention Invested 54

9 Policies and Procedures 55
Schedule 55
    Sales Concerns 55
    Large Volume Production
        Concerns 56
    Preparing the Clients 56
Prepare 57
    Housekeeping 57
    Standard Supplies 58
    Strategize 58
Conduct 60
    Introduction 61
    Agenda 61
        Assumptions 61
        Budget 61
        Change Requests 62
        Quality 62
        Site Visits 62
        Something's Missing 63
    Conclusion 63
Follow Through 63

10 Predictable Situations 64
Change Requests 64
Checkbook Amnesia 65
Delivery Date 65
Error in Paperwork 65
Incomplete Selections 66
Site-Related Issues 66
Surprise Issues 67

PART 4 Frame Stage Tour 69
Quality Inside the Walls

11 Policies and Procedures 71
Schedule 71

Prepare 72
Conduct 72
    Introduction 74
    Agenda 74
    Conclusion 74
Follow Through 75

12 Predictable Situations 76
Buyers Expect an Item
    Not Ordered 76
Buyers' Lists 76
Buyers Live Out of State 77
Change Requests 77
Error in the Home 78
Quality Debate 78
Trades 78

PART 5 Home Buyer Orientation 81
Golden Opportunity

Walking-Talking Billboard 81
Warranty Relationship 81
Transition from Buying to Owning 82

13 Policies and Procedures 83
Schedule 83
Prepare 84
Conduct 84
    Itinerary 85
        Begin at the Street 85
        Exterior First 86
        Front Entrance 86
        Kitchen Last 86
    Agenda 87
    Introduction 87
    Conclusion 91
    Techniques 92
        Upon (Early) Arrival 92
        Have Something to Say in
            Each Room 93
        Hands-On 93
        Volunteer Items 93
        Describe the Item 93
Follow Through 94

14 Predictable Situations 96
Buyers Arrive with a Ladder and a Flashlight 96
Buyers Arrive with a List 96
Buyers Refuse to Begin until a Third Party Arrives 97
Closing Day Inspection 97
Construction Routinely Delivers Incomplete Homes 97
Escrow 98
Familiar Equals Right 98
Hidden Agenda 99
Home Inspector's List 99
Home Is Not Ready 99
I'm Not Closing Unless . . . 99
I'm Paying $X for This House 100
Inclement Weather 100
Item Reported by Home Buyers, Not Yet Corrected 100
I Used to Be in Construction 101
Latent Expectations 101
Monthly, Quarterly, or Year-End Crunch 101
Nit-Picking 102
Work from a Position of Strength 102
Technical Expert 102
Time Out 102
Leave Well-Enough Alone 102
Noise 103
No Showhome 103
Sales Moves Closing Dates 103
This House Isn't Built According to Code 103
Time Is Running Out 104
Triangles 104
Why Don't We Have . . . ? 104

PART 6 Warranty Service 107
Last, But Not Least

15 Policies and Procedures 109
Schedule 109
Control Your Part 109
Scheduling Inspection Appointments 110
Builder-Initiated Appointments 111
Appointments 111
Inspection Checklist 112
Confirmation 112
Prepare 112
Homeowner Manual 112
Avoid Prior Conclusions 115
Third Party Support 115
Conduct 115
Follow Through 117
Enforcing Time Frames 117
Tracking Items 119
Computer Support 119
Manual Systems 119
Closure 121
Confirm Satisfaction 121

16 Predictable Situations 122
Access 122
Keys or Appointments? 122
Key Release 123
Homeowner Temporarily Unavailable 123
Additional Items 123
Alternative Dispute Resolution 123
Angry Letter 124
Consumer Protection Entities 125
Cosmetic Damage 125
Defective Material 126
Difference in Standards 127
Drama 128
Extended Hours 128
Exterior Work 129
Homeowner's Possessions 129
I Didn't Buy a Patched House 130
Cosmetic 130
Practical 130
Psychological 130
I Don't Care What Your Manual Says 131
I Paid $X for This House 131
I've Already Talked to My Attorney 131
I Want a Copy of Everything in the Warranty File 131

I Want to Talk to the Owner **132**
Legal Action Pending **132**
Listing Agent List **132**
Media **132**
Method of Repair **133**
Missed Appointments **134**
Orientation Items Incomplete or
Unacceptable **134**
Out of Warranty **135**
  Grace Period **135**
  Code Items **135**
  Contract Items **135**
  Latent Defect **135**
  Written Notice **136**
  Recurring Items **136**
  Manufacturer Covered Claims **136**
Pets **136**
Repetitious Requests **136**

Requests to Non-Warranty
Personnel **137**
Retirees: At Home and Away **138**
  What's Your Hurry? **138**
  I'm on a Fixed Income **138**
  I'll Die in This House **138**
  New Fangled Gizmos **138**
  Part Time Occupants **139**
  Full Time Examination **139**
  Maintenance Options **139**
Revenge List **139**
Roof Leaks **139**
Second Owners **140**
Signature Negotiations **142**
Wet Basement **142**

Conclusion 144

Resources 145

List of Figures

Part 1. Knowledge Is Power
The Raw Material of Service

Chapter 1. Community

1.1   Community Inventory 8

Chapter 2. Company

2.1   Procedure Review 10
2.2   Sales Presentation: Key Points 11
2.3   Purchase Agreement: Key Points 12
2.4   Mortgage Terms 12
2.5   Selections and Change Orders: Key Points 13
2.6   Preconstruction Conference: Key Points 14
2.7   Frame Stage Tour: Key Points 14
2.8   Orientation: Key Points 15
2.9   Closing: Key Points 15
2.10   Warranty Repair Appointment: Key Points 16
2.11   Company Reports: Key Points 16

Chapter 3. Home Construction

3.1   Home Construction Review 18

Chapter 4. Product Profile

4.1   Product Profile Review 21

Chapter 5. Maintenance and Warranty

5.1   Maintenance and Warranty: Components and Systems 24
5.2   Maintenance and Warranty: Component Review 25

Part 2. The Meetings
Common Elements and
Uncommon Skills

Chapter 7. Attitudes, Communication Skills, and Habits That Help

7.1   Incident Report 40

Part 3. Preconstruction Conference
Expectations for the Building
Process

Chapter 9. Policies and Procedures

9.1   Sample Preconstruction Conference Agenda: Custom 59
9.2   Sample Preconstruction Conference Agenda: Production 60

Part 4. Frame Stage Tour
Quality Inside the Walls

Chapter 11. Policies and Procedures

11.1   Sample Frame Stage Tour Agenda 73

Part 5. Home Buyer Orientation
Golden Opportunity

Chapter 13. Policies and Procedures

13.1   Sample Orientation Agenda 88
13.2   Sample Orientation Introduction 91
13.3   Sample Orientation Conclusion 92

Part 6. Warranty Service
Last, But Not Least

Chapter 15. Policies and Procedures

15.1   Builder Initiated Warranty Inspection 113
15.2   Warranty Service Request 114
15.3   Warranty Inspection 116
15.4   Sample Warranty Work Order 118
15.5   Sample Work Order Log 120

Chapter 16. Predictable Situations

16.1   Leak Follow-Up 141
16.2   Wet Basement 143

Carol Smith's Customer Relations Series

Customer service is one person doing something for one other person—whether that other person is a paying customer, a coworker, or an associate. This Customer Relations Series offers tools and techniques for improving all types of customer relationships. To achieve that goal, this series examines many aspects of homebuilding and remodeling.

Virtually anyone who has contact with customers of any type will benefit from this series. Our audience includes homebuilding firms of all sizes, remodelers, trade contractors, salespeople, suppliers, mortgage professionals, real estate agents, interior designers, architects, engineers, inspectors, and others.

Book topics include all phases of the homebuilding or remodeling relationship: from sales through construction, from delivery through warranty, and from feedback to improvement. We believe that quality management principles apply to the process as well as they do to the product. By listening to customers, defining the ideal, measuring the real, and noticing the difference, professionals improve.

Our constant objective is to identify and present a balanced view of customer relations issues, thereby allowing an informed audience to make informed decisions. Many right ways of serving customers exist. The challenge is to identify and excel in the combination that is right for each company or individual. This series intends to help you do just that. Customer relations improves your reputation and results in satisfied customers, referrals, and repeat clients.

About the Author and Series Editor

Carol Smith is the leading customer relations expert for home builders. Her 30 years of front-line experience with customers are immediately apparent in her realistic and practical approach to the issue of meetings with clients. She has performed over 700 buyer orientations, held the posts of superintendent, customer home sales manager, and vice president of customer relations. In 1999 she founded Customer Relations Professionals (CRP), and international association that provides education and recognition to customer service professionals.

Since 1986 Smith has presented hundreds of educational programs to builders, associates, and others in the United States and abroad, including NAHB's International Builders' Show, regional conferences, seminars sponsored by the Home Builders' Institute (HBI), Custom Builder Symposium, and others, She developed the curriculum for the Home Builders Institute's full-day Customer Service course. (Many of these seminars are now under the aegis of the University of Housing.)

Carol has written numerous successful books, including *Building Your Home: An Insider's Guide,* 2nd ed.; *Customer Service for home Builders, Dear homeowner: A Book of Customer Service Letters, homeowner Manual: A Template for home Builders,* 2nd ed.; *Warranty Service for home Builders.*

She started her newsletter, *Home Address,* in 1986 for builders. In the spring of 2006, she launches *Home Address: Welcome Home,* A free online newsletter for consumers. For more information see her web site www.cjsmithhomeaddress.com.

Smith is an award-winning columnist for *Custom Home* magazine and has written dozens of articles for such publications as *Builders Management Journal, Premier Homes, Building Homes and Profits,* and *Builder* magazine.

She has been a licensed Colorado real estate broker since 1988.

Acknowledgments

Reviewers

BuilderBooks would like to thank the following people for reviewing the outline and/or manuscript for *Meetings with Clients: A Self-Study Manual for a Builder's Front-Line Personnel*: Barbie Lussier, Lussier Construction, Cameron Park, CA and Bob Whitten, Cooper Homes, Bella Vista, AR.

Introduction
How to Use This Guide

Most of us have experienced job training with the folklore approach—traditions. These traditions, as interpreted by the trainer (someone who used to do the job) are passed from employee to employee. This works for some tasks, and the resulting performance may even be acceptable to customers. Although book "learnin'" helps, it won't tell you how to deal with a client who is irate over a careless remark made by a trade contractor's employee. A lot can be said for real-world experience, but hand-me-down training carries a risk. Each time information is passed along, some things may be omitted; points not intended by the company may be added to the training curriculum; and the attitudes conveyed will be influenced by the trainer's bias.

Without discounting the value of folklore training, we should also recognize that first-hand investigation offers significant benefits. Increase your knowledge of home buyers and build self confidence by using a comprehensive approach that systematically investigates the many aspects of the new home experience. This Guide provides tools and information to organize and support your efforts in this area.

The materials in this Guide will help you understand attitudes, increase your knowledge of home buyers, and polish your communication skills to succeed in working with home buyers.

This Guide includes three elements: (1) raw material that anyone working for a home builder should be learning, (2) detailed analysis of four common builder-hosted meetings that ensure home buyer satisfaction, and (3) insights into the folklore (see "Predictable Situations").

Raw Material

Part 1 contains worksheets that will help you gather information. Make an appropriate number of copies of each worksheet and keep the originals for future use. Next, organize your worksheets in a file or notebook. This way, you can act on many of the worksheet items immediately. Completing all the entries will include tasks such as reading manufacturer brochures, interviewing colleagues, visiting places, trying out appliances, or practicing by role playing in difficult conversations.

As you progress, some activities will overlap, and the information may intertwine. For instance, you may interview a superintendent in your research about construction and later find that you can refer to those notes when you study the community in which that superintendent builds. Or you might collect literature about area schools that will enable you to pass along an update to a sales person with whom you interview.

The time required to complete your self-managed course will vary. Naturally, the more time you invest, the faster your effort will generate rewards. The flexible nature of the Guide allows you to work on more than one topic at a time, progress at your pace, and return to complete new worksheets later, if conditions change.

Because the worksheets are comprehensive, you might ask "Why do I need to know about this? I don't work in sales/mortgages/selections/construction/orientation/warranty." One of the objectives of this Guide is to give you a clear view of the proverbial "big picture," and at the same time, refine your specific performance skills. You will be surprised at how often seemingly extraneous information is useful in your work. You may even discover a new aspect of the home building industry that will lead to an unexpected career opportunity.

One last tip, before getting started, think about where you will keep the materials you collect (maps, brochures, floor plans, handouts, forms, and warranties) and how you will organize them. A file drawer, closet, bookshelf, binders, and wall charts may be part of your plan. Well-organized, these materials will be handy references and can be updated easily.

Client Meetings

Part 2 includes a discussion about client meetings and begins with some general tips. In this Part, you will find suggestions that apply to all meetings with clients. Next, in chronological order, Parts 3 through 6 address each of four specific client meetings:

1. Preconstruction Conference
2. Frame Stage Tour
3. Homeowner Orientation
4. Warranty Inspection

Policies and Procedures

Typical policies and procedures for conducting each type of meeting are reviewed. The policies and procedures in this Part include several questions that will help you assess your company's methods. By answering these questions, you will discover how your company manages their clients from beginning to end. You may find these questions highlight areas that could be improved, uncover contradictions, or identify inconsistencies.

Predictable Situations

Each Part concludes with "Predictable Situations," which includes an alphabetical list of common challenges and common sense responses. Although these predictable situations are organized according to the meeting in which they are most likely to occur, some of the described behaviors may cross the arbitrary boundaries I've imposed.

You may find it useful to review, at least briefly, the Predictable Situations in all Parts even though you may not be involved currently in these types of meetings. As you consider these real-world scenarios, you will find you are not alone in facing the challenges of today's home buyers. With this manual, you can turn those challenges into successes.

Terminology

The meetings and the personnel described in this manual may go by other names in your company. For instance, the Frame Stage Tour is often referred to as a Pre-drywall Walk. The phrase "orientation rep" refers to the person who conducts the orientation; not every home building company will have that position or use that title. The business card of the person who conducts orientations in your company may read "Warranty Manager," "Superintendent," or "Customer Service Rep." Regardless of meeting names or job titles, the skills listed in this Guide will lead to superior performance and satisfied clients.

Diskette

All of the forms and checklists included in this manual appear on a diskette bound into the inside back cover. The figure numbers in the manual identify the figures on the disk. If necessary, you can convert these Microsoft Word files with any compatible word processing software.

Knowledge Is Power
The Raw Material of Service

When you are unsure of what to say or do for a client, lack of knowledge may be the cause of your discomfort. If you have solid information and know where to go for more, you can handle any situation confidently. By working through the exercises in this Guide, you will acquire considerable knowledge and create a network of professionals to whom you can turn to for additional information and support. Whatever job you hold within your company, you should be familiar with the following:

- Communities in which your company builds
- Your company's operations: policies, procedures, and communication network (meetings and reports)
- Technical aspects of home construction in your region
- Your company's products and available variations
- Typical home maintenance tasks and your company's limited warranty guidelines

As you explore these five areas, the checklists and worksheets that follow will help you stay organized and allow you to track your progress. Add other topics you believe deserve your study. For instance, large companies may have land development, architectural, purchasing, estimating, closing, or human resources departments. If this is the case, take time to learn the "who, what, where, when, and how" of each of these functions—at least in general. The read-interview-observe approach expands easily to include diverse areas. When complete, you will have a valuable reference library of notes and materials.

1

Community

Invest the time to learn the streets and visit the services that are available in the communities in which your company builds. Use Figure 1.1, Community Inventory, as a starting point. Check off each category as you complete your review and add others as they occur. Visit the zoo, ride on the public bus or monorail, shop at the mall, see a movie, and spend time in local schools. You might need to play a round of golf, walk through a local park, and enjoy a few meals at area restaurants. How else can you talk to interested clients intelligently about such things?

As you explore, gather brochures and other materials about the area for your resource files. Sources include chambers of commerce, county extension services, tourist bureaus, recreation centers, and libraries. Some of these items may be useful to new homeowners in your area.

Years ago, when I conducted home buyer orientations in the Denver area, I kept a supply of booklets titled, "Cooking at High Altitude," and offered one to each home buyer who was moving from an area with a lower altitude. Create a supply of relevant materials to add to the standard materials that your company provides to clients. As part of your community exploration, visit the homes of other builders. Knowing what the competition is doing and what features and quality are available in our marketplace can be helpful.

FIGURE 1.1 Community Inventory

☐ **Map**—Get to know the streets and highways. Are there "back ways" a driver can take to avoid rush-hour traffic?

☐ **Emergency services**—What jurisdiction provides fire, police, and poison control services?

☐ **Hospitals**—Which have emergency facilities?

☐ **Government offices**—Locate driver's license office, voter registration, and post office.

☐ **Shops, shopping centers, and malls**—Note locations of major chains and unusual independent merchants.

☐ **Transportation**—What taxi, airport, bus, or rail services are available? Experience some of these for yourself.

☐ **Schools**—Visit them and learn about some of their programs.

☐ **Places of worship**—Note significant programs and locations.

☐ **Banking**—Locate main branches. Which banks have services in grocery stores?

☐ **Recreation facilities**—Swim in the pool, take a pottery class, go on a picnic.

☐ **Newspapers**—What's available: daily? weekly? How are they delivered?

☐ **Trash collection**—Which days of the week? Time of day? Are there any special procedures?

☐ **Recycling**—Where and how is it available?

☐ **Utility companies**—How do homeowners get underground lines marked? Are conservation tips available?

☐ **Cable TV**—What is the current status or lead time for connection?

☐ **What hi-speed, hi-tech services are available?**

☐ **Who are your competitors? What do they offer?**

Other: _____

_____

Company

Familiarity with company policies, procedures, and lines of authority is fundamental to job success. This holds true regardless of the size of the company or where you work in the organization. Issues may arise that are best resolved with a sales professional. Others may be settled with the construction or land development groups. Review the organizational chart for your company. Learn who's who and how people and departments relate to each other—formally and informally. Become familiar with how your company manages all aspects of the new home process.

For each of these topics (and those you add) go through a three-step review: (1) read related printed materials (contracts, agreements, addenda, forms, brochures, information sheets), (2) interview those in your company who perform the various processes, and (3) observe one or more appointments with actual clients. The worksheet in Figure 2.1, Procedure Review, provides a cover sheet for your notes on each topic.

During your interviews with company personnel and appointments with clients, ask yourself what key points need to be covered, and what possible confusions might arise? What are the challenges that must be met to succeed? Understand the reasons for company procedures and learn how the procedures are explained to home buyers. What exceptions, if any, are possible? When you hear client concerns, you will be ready to respond accurately or know whom to go to for assistance. When you do not know the answer to a client's question, knowing who to ask is the next best service you can provide.

A list of typical builder procedures and points of which to be aware are outlined in Figure 2.1. Of course, another way to learn these points is to buy a home from your company and experience these procedures personally.

Sales Presentation

In addition to interviewing one or more sales people, eavesdrop on several sales presentations to prospective home buyers. To prepare for this, review your company's advertising. This might include newspaper ads, local housing publications, or even television spots. Visit the company website to see what buyers see. Note signs that direct prospects to the

FIGURE 2.1 Procedure Review

Procedure _____

☐ **Documentation.** Gather copies of the documents related to this procedure, list them below, and check each one as you read it.

_____
_____
_____
_____
_____
_____
_____

☐ **Interviews.** Interview one or more individuals who work with clients to perform this procedure. Attach notes as needed.

Date   **Name**

_____   _____
_____   _____
_____   _____

☐ **Observations.** Observe one or more appointments with clients to see a real example of this procedure. Attach notes as needed.

Date   **Name**

_____   _____
_____   _____
_____   _____

☐ **Conclusions.** Record your thoughts and conclusions regarding this procedure. What are the strengths? Where are the opportunities to improve this part of the new home process in your company? Attach your notes to this sheet.

sales center. Study the sales brochure, floor plans, displays, and handouts available from the sales center. What impression do these materials make?

Spend time in the sales office during a busy day. Follow along, observing and listening. Note how the sales person greets prospective buyers, discovers their needs, and presents information about the builder, the community, and the product. A good sales person makes this look easy. Try it yourself, and you will learn it takes considerable training and practice.

FIGURE 2.2 Sales Presentation: Key Points

- How are prospects greeted?

- Do prospects complete a guest card?

- What questions does the sales person ask?

- What information does the sales person give?

- Does the sales person accompany them through the showhomes?

- Does the presentation include the choices that are available, delivery times, limited warranty, or the company homeowner manual?

- How are optional or upgraded items that are displayed in showhomes identified for prospects?

- Listen for information about the client's needs and expectations.

- Does the sales person take notes?

- How will these early conversations impact the relationship with these prospective buyers if they decide to purchase?

- If you were in the market for a new home, what would stand out in your mind from this presentation?

- What else would you appreciate or want to hear about?

Contract Session: Purchase Agreement

In your interviews with sales people, ask which community issues, product features, or contract clauses they think need extra attention to prevent misunderstandings. Read the entry in your homeowner manual to see what your company tells home buyers about the purchase agreement. Notice how your company's homeowner manual is presented and used during this meeting.

Because the purchase agreement and related materials are so detailed and important to everything that follows, understand your company's purchase agreement, especially the clauses on topics such as those listed in Figure 2.3.

Keep in mind that each subdivision may also have various addenda and disclosures unique to its circumstances. At the end of the presentation, does the sales person prepare the client for the next steps in the process (financing and selections)? If your company offers design/build or sweat equity services, apply this same level of study to the design agreement.

Mortgage Application

Sitting through a loan application appointment with an actual buyer may be awkward because so much personal information is discussed. Instead, you may prefer to meet with a loan officer and have him or her walk you through the process as if you were applying for a mortgage. Review related documents and discuss typical issues that come up just as you did with the sales people.

FIGURE 2.3 Purchase Agreement: Key Points

- Price of the home
- Allowances
- Reimbursable expenses
- Financing
- Commence and complete construction
- Change orders
- Conformance with plans and specifications
- Plan ownership
- Site visits
- Noninterference
- Inspection and acceptance
- Site clean-up

- Mandatory clauses (insulation, radon)
- Warranty
- Settlement
- Possession
- Default or termination
- Alternative dispute resolution (ADR)
- Co-op broker
- Homeowners association
- Documents
- Dues
- Design review guidelines

In addition to a familiarity with the standard forms and an understanding of basic mortgage terminology such as those listed in Figure 2.4, watch for aspects of the borrowing process that might frustrate clients and come up in your contacts with home buyers. These might include an underwriter's request for last minute documentation, shock over the final closing figures, or difficulty resolving a loan contingency.

FIGURE 2.4 Mortgage Terms

- Application
- Loan-to-value ratio
- Debt ratio
- Mortgage ratio
- Verification of Deposit
- Verification of Employment
- Verification of Mortgage
- Truth in Lending
- Good Faith Estimate
- Origination fee
- Points
- Mortgage insurance
- Interest rate
- Lock

- Contingency
- Hazard insurance escrow
- Property tax escrow
- Buy down
- Down payment
- Monthly principal and interest
- Adjustable rate mortgage
- Fixed rate mortgage
- Conventional
- FHA
- VA
- Underwriting
- Contingency

Selections

The selection process has received considerable attention in recent years. In fact, today's home buyers have more choices than ever. Many companies have free-standing design centers that offer one-stop shopping for busy clients and provide a central location to display most of the products and colors that are available. Because these design centers are staffed by in-house personnel, builders have better control over the information home buyers receive, and company procedures are more readily followed.

Even without a company design center, the selection process no doubt plays a larger role in your company's buying process than in past years. After reading the available selections in your homeowner manual and reviewing the forms used in the selection process, select one or two buyers and follow them through their selection appointments. In particular, note how home buyers proceed within your company's time frames. If applicable, follow a custom change request from start to finish, including the pricing process. Experiencing the life cycle of a custom change order will help you see how misunderstandings can occur. The practical details to cover in this process are listed in Figure 2.5.

Preconstruction Conference

If your company conducts preconstruction conferences, attend one. Note the contributions made by the sales person and the superintendent. Are trust and confidence in the superintendent established? How? These sessions intend to review all plans and specifications, selections, and change orders for the new home. Details are double-checked to ensure that all parties are working off the same page.

Buyer expectations about the building process should be aligned with potential realities. For more details see Part 3 and check your company's homeowner manual to see how it prepares home buyers for this meeting. In your review of this meeting, look for answers to questions such as those listed in Figure 2.6.

FIGURE 2.5 Selections and Change Orders: Key Points

- Where do home buyers go to make their selections?

- What are the hours?

- Who staffs the facility?

- Are appointments needed?

- Is browsing time available?

- Is the homeowner manual displayed and available as a reference?

- Do home buyers sign each page of their selections?

- What, if any, disclaimers might be included?

- Do home buyers receive samples of colors they select?

- What deadlines or cut-offs apply?

- Are change orders accepted?

- Are all changes documented?

- How long does pricing take on a custom change order?

- Does a design deposit apply to custom changes?

- Does an administrative fee apply to change orders?

FIGURE 2.6 Preconstruction Conference: Key Points

- Where is this meeting held?
- Who is expected to attend?
- How long does this meeting last?
- How is this meeting introduced?
- Is there a printed agenda?
- How is the homeowner manual incorporated into the meeting?
- How are requests for more changes to the plans or specifications handled?
- How is the meeting concluded?
- What follow-up steps ensure that buyer questions are answered?
- What circumstances might get the home buyer off track at this point?
- What problems can be prevented by the preconstruction conference?

Frame Stage Tour

Also called the predrywall walk, the frame stage tour is an official home buyer visit to the site. These tours usually involve the home buyers and the superintendent and are the shortest of the preclosing meetings with home buyers. Visible options and change order items should be confirmed, and the quality that goes inside the walls of the homes should be pointed out to the buyers.

Just as one of the objectives of the preconstruction conference was to create confidence in the superintendent, this meeting should generate confidence in the home. Questions to consider are listed in Figure 2.7.

Home Buyer Orientation

Home buyer orientations usually take from 90 minutes to 2 hours, but can go much longer depending on the buyers and the size (and condition) of the home. Block out sufficient time to observe the entire meeting. Prepare by studying the forms that will be used and reviewing the documentation from several previous orientations. While observing the orientations, keep the key points in Figure 2.8 in mind.

FIGURE 2.7 Frame Stage Tour: Key Points

- How is this meeting introduced?
- What itinerary is followed?
- Is there a written agenda of points to cover?
- What information does the homeowner manual include about this meeting?
- How is the homeowner manual incorporated into the meeting?
- Notice the cleanliness of the home, the site, and the general area. What impression is the company making?
- How is the meeting concluded?
- What issues might arise as a result of the frame stage tour?
- What problems can be prevented?

FIGURE 2.8 Orientation: Key Points

- Did the orientation representative arrive before the home buyers?

- What preparation steps does the orientation representative make?

- Take special note of how the home buyers are greeted.

- How is this meeting introduced? Concluded?

- Does the agenda emphasize education or inspection?

- Is the home ready to present–complete and clean?

- How will the orientation influence the buyers' attitudes toward the company during the warranty period?

Closing

Although the closing or settlement on a home purchase usually takes about an hour, it is an intense hour. Most of the documentation is mysterious to home buyers. Signatures are required on about 75 documents, many of which are duplicates because several entities receive copies. In your interview with the closing agent, ask for brief explanations of the basic documents.

Work with clients who have enjoyed your company in earlier appointments. Notice the tasks that the buyers need to complete in preparation for closing: arranging for utility transfer, obtaining hazard insurance on the new home, removing any loan contingencies, and securing funds for the final payment. These should be listed in your company's home-owner manual. In addition, consider how the closing agent handles the meeting by noting the answers to the questions listed in Figure 2.9.

Warranty Service

Procedures for obtaining warranty service, the builder's guidelines for screening warranty items, and normal home maintenance tasks should be described clearly in the homeowner manual. After reviewing that material, follow along on several warranty inspections and notice how expectations created earlier in the buying process (beginning in the sales office) impact the tone and outcome of these meetings.

Interview warranty staff members about quality standards and any procedural issues that cause friction with homeowners. How are expectations about the repair process set? How are service denials handled?

FIGURE 2.9 Closing: Key Points

- Are the buyers greeted and made to feel welcome upon their arrival?

- Is the closing process started promptly and is it well organized?

- Is a representative from your company present?

- How are questions handled?

- Is a thank-you gift included in the proceedings?

- Is a buyer satisfaction survey part of the paperwork?

- What is the general tone? This should be a happy event for the home buyers.

FIGURE 2.10   Warranty Repair Appointment: Key Points

- Is the technician on time for the appointment?

- Is the work completed efficiently?

- Is the work area cleaned up?

- Does the homeowner sign the work order when the work is complete?

- What special challenges do the warranty technicians (in-house or trade contractor) face?

To be thorough, select one or two of the inspections that you observed and visit those homes when the resulting warranty work is performed. Take note of the items in Figure 2.10.

Company Meetings and Reports

You have completed a whirlwind tour of what it is like to buy a home from your company. Next, turn your attention to the behind-the-scenes company communication system that makes all of this happen. Sit in on at least one of each routine meeting. Who meets, how often, when, and where? Does each group have a standard agenda of items to review? (How might you get a topic of yours on one of these agendas?) Routine meetings fall into the following categories:

- Management team (department heads)
- Departmental (all sales, all construction, or all warranty staff)
- Community (sales, superintendent, and warranty meet on site to review all buyer files—usually weekly)

Another possible meeting that is likely to be irregular but is worth observing is the hiring and indoctrination of a new trade contractor. How much attention is devoted to client service and warranty procedures during this meeting? Are copies of forms reviewed and standards of behavior for client interactions discussed?

Add to your survey of meetings a review of the company's reporting systems. Learn what standard reports are issued by each function or department. As applicable, answer the questions listed in Figure 2.11.

FIGURE 2.11   Company Reports: Key Points

- What company function is the report about?

- What things does the report measure?

- At what interval?

- What is the cutoff for data included?

- When is the report due?

- Are report formats logical and consistent?

- Who compiles the report?

- Who receives the report?

- When will the report be discussed?

- What results are expected?

Home Construction

A general understanding of how a house is built is fundamental to your work with home buyers. Learn how your company puts a home together—first on paper, and then, in reality. With this technical knowledge, you can resolve many client questions on the spot, which reduces follow-up time and raises your home buyer's comfort level.

Visit the field often, even if you are a veteran at your job. Ideally, select a home to watch from start to finish. This means frequent visits to the site to see each phase of the work. Talk with trades people and the superintendent; ask questions until you understand what you are seeing.

Particular weather or other natural conditions are unique to each region. Such conditions can be alarming to home buyers who are new to your area. An understanding of specific regional factors—soil conditions, termites, or potential weather or seismic events—and how to talk about them to buyers can be vital. Know when to consult another expert so you do not mislead a buyer unintentionally.

Carry a camera and keep a log of what you photograph and when and where you took each picture. This will be valuable for later review. A person cannot know everything about construction. However, an organized investigation will help you establish a framework of knowledge quickly, ensuring your success, and increasing your value to your company. Interview those involved or observe the steps listed in Figure 3.1, making appropriate adjustments for your company's products.

Reading for this aspect of client meetings may be extensive if your company is one that uses detailed contracts and scopes of work with trades. What documents do home buyers receive (floor plans, specifications) and what does the homeowner manual explain about the construction process?

FIGURE 3.1 Home Construction Review

Item	Date/Location	Photo #
☐ Safety manual		
☐ Design		
☐ Engineering		
☐ Permitting		
☐ Purchasing and purchase orders		
☐ Trade contracts and scopes of work		
☐ Construction scheduling and updating		
☐ Building department inspections		
☐ Change order processing		
☐ Stake out		
☐ Excavation		
☐ Foundation		
☐ Waterproof and drain line		
☐ Framing		
☐ Roof		
☐ Exterior trim		
☐ Exterior finish		
☐ Grading		
☐ Flatwork		
☐ Landscaping		
☐ Mechanicals (rough stage)		
• Plumbing		
• Heating		
• Electrical		
☐ Insulation		
☐ Drywall		
☐ Interior trim		
☐ Paint/stain		
☐ Cabinets		
☐ Counters		
☐ Tile		
☐ Floor coverings		
☐ Mechanicals (finish stage)		
• Plumbing		
• Heating		
• Electrical		
☐ Hardware		
☐ Punchlist		
☐ Cleaning		
☐ Orientation and completion of items		

4

Product Profile

To judge anything, you must first know the standard. Knowing your company's floor plans and standard and optional features will help you respond to questions, such as "Shouldn't this closet have another shelf?"

Spend time in each showhome. Then, go back and spend more time in them. If your company offers a floor plan that is not shown as a showhome, review one that is under construction. In each floor plan, look at every room from several angles. Look under and behind items. How are the bottoms of window sills finished? Does the paint on the backs of by-pass closet doors look any different from the front? Study the details thoroughly enough that you can envision each room and how the details are finished. Next, walk the exterior. Learn to recognize the available elevations and what each includes.

Create a notebook or file of information about each subdivision or product line. Using Figure 4.1 as a guide, keep the following items in mind.

Standard House

Buyers can easily become confused about what is standard in their floor plans. Seeing past the decorator items and keeping track of builder-added options and upgrades can be difficult. Because questions are guaranteed, know which features are standard and which are extras—or at least know how to find answers quickly. This information can change, especially as market conditions fluctuate, so review the list with sales and construction regularly.

Changes in Production: Substituting "Equal or Better"

Once the showhomes open and the construction begins, the homes being built will evolve while the showhomes remain static. Suppliers change, appliance manufacturers update features, and a new trade contractor or a different crew may do future work slightly differently than the former one. Many savvy companies study the nature and number of warranty items and make changes in its construction practices to prevent recurrences. This process is natural and often unavoidable.

However, home buyers may become disgruntled if they do not receive exactly what they saw in the showhome. Pointing to the contract clause that gives builders the right to make changes is a weak defense from a customer's perspective.

To minimize these types of problems, construction should inform sales, selections, the orientation rep, and warranty when significant materials or methods change. Regular meetings, departmental reports, routine review of showhomes, and written notice of changes help to keep this under control.

Slight Variations

Because homes are handcrafted products, no two are exactly alike. Yet, when light switches, heat vents, and the like are not precisely in the same spot as in the showhome, some home buyers object. Prepare them for this type of change. Likewise, details in the home can vary due to topography, soil conditions, code revisions, and changes in homeowner association design requirements. Understand any circumstance that can cause changes, and know what sales people (and your homeowner manual) tell home buyers on this subject.

Options and Upgrades

Home buyers can be confused if they are unclear about how an option or upgrade will look or what it will include. The classic example is rough-in plumbing in basements. Builders sell this option; then, install basic ground plumbing and some pipes in the basement. Buyers expect something much closer to a finished bathroom. When possible, review the actual item and all that it includes so you can answer questions. Minimally, study the written description and know where to go for more details in case questions arise.

Custom Changes

Because clients invest extra time and money in custom changes, they pay particular attention to the results. Their custom change may exist one way in their minds and appear another way in their finished home. To minimize such misunderstandings, every change should be documented with a detailed description on a change order and supplemented with drawings or diagrams, catalog pages, and photos, where appropriate.

Handouts and Displays

Many companies supplement their showhomes with displays and handouts in the sales office. These might highlight product features or promote the builder and the community. Typically you will find topo tables, artist renderings, wall displays, brochures, single-sheet handouts, and so on. Like the showhomes, these materials usually do not change while the homes under construction may evolve. Developer commitments for amenities such as tennis courts and pools as well as plans for the surrounding land are also likely to be topics of conversation or written materials found in the sales office.

Be familiar with the information that home buyers see or receive. You may hear comments or complaints about these details from clients. For instance, if the developer does not build the pool on time, homeowners can—with justification—become very angry. Respond appropriately and know who to contact for the current information and support. Also, as you review these materials, watch for contradictions in information. If you discover something that could cause confusion with buyers, alert the appropriate person.

FIGURE 4.1 Product Profile Review

Community: _____

Location: _____

Directions: _____

On-Site Personnel	Sales	Construction
Name(s)		
Phone		
Mobile Phone		
Fax		
E-mail		

Floor Plan*	Base Price	Sq ft	Comments

*Attach 8½ × 11 floor plans if available

Community Data

☐ Number of homes at completion

☐ Date community opened

☐ Anticipated close-out date

☐ Merchandising (brochures, feature lists, etc.)

☐ Purchase agreement and addenda

☐ Option list

☐ Selection sheet

☐ Change order policy and change order form

☐ Homeowner manual

☐ Homeowner association documents

Tour Showhomes

Date _____

Date _____

Date _____

Date _____

Date _____

Date _____

5

Maintenance and Warranty

Component by component—beginning with standard items and working through options and common upgrades—learn all you can about each material or product that your company includes in its homes. Study use and care, troubleshooting, and long-term expectations for each item.

Begin with a list of the components or systems that you need to review. For each, anticipate questions and concerns. For example, regarding front doors, what questions might a client ask? What complaints are typical? Some of the following issues might be discussed.

- Real wood doors may respond to changes in temperature and humidity.
- Metal doors can be dented; do not kick them open because your arms are full of packages.
- Dark-colored doors exposed to the sun may require extra maintenance.
- Is the threshold adjustable? If so, how?
- Magnetic weather stripping may mar the paint on metal doors.
- What insulation properties does the door have?
- Demonstrate the lock and deadbolt function, making certain the deadbolt engages fully.
- Are deadbolt and door lock keys the same?
- When, where, and from whom will the home buyers receive their keys?
- Who else, if anyone, will have a key once the home buyers close on their new home?

Proceed in this manner through all home components. This is initially time consuming. However, you will benefit from this knowledge in caring for your home. Learn from many sources; stay alert for new information. Many supplemental resources are available.

Building Codes

Classes are often available covering applicable codes for a region; you may want to sign up for one. At the least, know which building department has jurisdiction over each of your company's construction sites or subdivisions. Look through a current code book. Review the table of contents and read several entries to understand how the information is organized and what level of detail is included. Know who to contact with questions about code requirements.

Manufacturer's and Supplier's Literature

Read the booklets and paperwork that come with standard appliances, furnaces, water heaters, and so on. Go to a showhome or a home under construction, and take yourself through routine tasks such as setting clocks, removing parts for cleaning, and replacing filters or batteries. Your experience using each item may generate some questions for further research.

Talk with installers or suppliers. Some manufacturers want to meet with builder employees for a training session about their products. Their information is valuable, and you can add manufacturers to your network of contacts. Visit supplier showrooms and chat with sales people there. Listen to feedback from company personnel and homeowners (often the most valuable source of all).

Homeowner Manual

Be familiar with your company's homeowner manual so you can reference it often. This establishes its authority in buyers' minds. If you can find printed information on specific topics quickly, you will establish credibility with home buyers. Read this material from beginning to end every 6 months. Start a file of notes for future revisions. Write your ideas down. A comprehensive and well-written homeowner manual must be kept current to make everyone's job easier and satisfy clients.

Builder Limited Warranty

Like maintenance information, review the terms of the limited warranty and related warranty guidelines regularly. If your company provides an insured warranty for homeowners, the same applies to that paperwork. Read, study, ask questions. Then, read it all again.

When buyer questions arise, go to the original sources. Read the documents for answers. Memory is an imperfect tool; support it with the hard copy. Over time, revisions do occur, and as with the details of construction, it may be a challenge to remember the updates. Learn about your state's statutes regarding builder warranty. Publications from your local home builders association sometimes include any updates.

Trade Shows, Conferences, Seminars

As a new home professional, attending regional and national programs may be part of your future. To get the most from such events, review the registration materials carefully and develop a list of seminars to attend and products to view (and wear comfortable shoes). You will see the latest innovations at such shows. Although your homes may not include them yet, a perspective on what's available is still useful. As a further benefit, meeting others in the home building industry at conferences adds to your support network.

You will probably not use every detail you learn from this extensive review with every client. However, strive to know more than you need. Then when a home buyer needs more than the basics, you'll be ready. Figure 5.1, Maintenance and Warranty Topics, and Figure 5.2, Maintenance and Warranty Worksheet, can help guide your research and organize your information.

FIGURE 5.1   Maintenance and Warranty: Components and Systems

☐ Air conditioning

☐ Appliances

☐ Asphalt

☐ Attic

☐ Brass fixtures

☐ Brick

☐ Cabinets

☐ Carpet

☐ Caulking

☐ Ceramic tile

☐ Concrete flatwork

☐ Condensation

☐ Countertops

☐ Crawl space

☐ Doors and locks

☐ Drywall

☐ Electrical

☐ Expansion and contraction

☐ Fireplace

☐ Foundation

☐ Garage overhead door

☐ Grading and drainage

☐ Gutters and downspouts

☐ Hardware

☐ Hardwood floors

☐ Heating system

☐ Humidifier

☐ Insulation

☐ Landscaping

☐ Mirrors

☐ Paint and stain

☐ Phone service

☐ Plumbing

☐ Resilient flooring

☐ Roof

☐ Rough carpentry

☐ Siding

☐ Smoke detectors

☐ Stairs and rails

☐ Stucco

☐ Vents

☐ Water heater

☐ Waterproofing

☐ Windows, screens, and sliding glass doors

☐ Wood trim

☐ Other

_____

_____

_____

_____

_____

FIGURE 5.2 Maintenance and Warranty: Component Review

Component or System_____

Standard Product _____

Options/Upgrades_____

_____

_____

_____

Function. Points to discuss, features to demonstrate

_____

_____

_____

Use and Care. Cleaning, routine maintenance, troubleshooting techniques

_____

_____

_____

Builder Limited Warranty. What does your company repair and what limitations apply?

_____

_____

_____

Manufacturer Warranty. Are there manufacturer protections beyond builder's warranty coverage?

_____

_____

_____

Experience. Feedback from homeowners, and so on

_____

_____

_____

Resources. Names, addresses, phone numbers _____

_____

_____

_____

The Meetings
Common Elements and Uncommon Skills

Today, builders recognize that customer service includes everything that happens between a client and the company. Everyone who works with or for clients affects what those clients think, feel, and say about the company, and therefore, can impact future business. This begins with the first phone call or visit and continues through the warranty period. To develop a positive service image, a builder must coordinate and control all phases of each client relationship. To this end, customer service comprises two main activities: initiating and reacting.

Initiating includes volunteering information, offering choices, providing updates, and inviting the clients to participate in meetings that keep them involved, informed, and comfortable. The parts of service the company initiates are deliberate. The personnel involved, content, and timing are all planned. The tone is usually positive.

Reacting includes the builder answering client questions, responding to complaints, and enforcing—when necessary—standards, procedures, and client responsibilities. Personnel involved, content, and timing are unpredictable. The tone is usually negative with causes ranging from simple mistakes or misunderstandings to outright conflict. Within a context of accurate information, regular communication, and growing trust, potentially negative occurrences are more readily resolved.

Both categories of service activities–initiating and reacting—require the knowledge and communication skills that you will acquire by using this Guide. There are four common types of home buyer meetings:

1. Preconstruction Conference
2. Frame Stage Tour
3. Home Buyer Orientation
4. Warranty Service

While each meeting contains its own particular points and potential issues, a common set of skills and attitudes contribute to success in all of them. This Part addresses those common elements. Likewise, in Chapter 8, Predictable Situations, you will find discussions of circumstances and occurrences that might be part of any client meeting.

6

Policies and Procedures

To avoid chaos, some practical decisions must be made by your company for each client meeting. These decisions form the frame work for the meetings, influence what training and preparation is appropriate, and determine what documentation will be needed. Typical decisions will include some of the following questions:

Location—Where will the meeting be held?

Attendees—Who will participate?

Agenda—What topics will be covered? A written agenda fosters consistency.

Policies—What policies apply to the typical issues that arise (for instance, home buyer change requests at the frame stage tour)?

You will want to be familiar with the answers to these questions as they apply to each client meeting. Think about managing each meeting in four steps: schedule, prepare, conduct, and follow-through.

Schedule

Scheduling may seem like an easy issue. The hectic pace of the today's world and the varying schedules of the meeting participants complicate this step. For instance, finding a time when the home buyers, the sales person, and the superintendent can get together for the preconstruction conference can be frustrating. Other duties of the participants, work schedules of your clients, and geography are just some of the factors to take into account when scheduling. Each community may have different scheduling parameters for its client meetings but will probably need to consider these questions:

- What event triggers the meeting? Paperwork that has been completed or a predetermined stage of work on the home may signal that the time has come to set up the next meeting.
- Who contacts the home buyers? This individual should use a checklist of reminders to help prepare the home buyers.

- What days and times are appointments available?
- How much notice should you provide to the clients for the appointment?
- How long should the meeting be expected to last?

Prepare

Preparation occurs in two steps: reviewing the client's file and talking with other company personnel who have worked with the clients. For example, in preparation for the frame stage tour, the superintendent should review the file and check with the sales person to see whether new issues have come up. The home buyers may be wondering about adding a fireplace, or they may have concerns about the target delivery date.

One objective of this step is to avoid making the clients re-tell their story. Seamless service means the company works to transfer information through the process on behalf of clients. Clients receive better care, and the home buyer who might attempt to play one staff member against another has less chance of success.

Knowing about any questions, even just one day prior to the meeting, allows the superintendent to check on the subject and, in many cases, have an answer at the meeting. If the home was to have a jetted tub and that tub is missing, you should know this before the meeting. Finally, this step allows company personnel to agree among themselves about how to respond to the client, thereby presenting consistent and more credible responses.

Predictions Versus Facts

Occasionally you will receive some advance evaluation from the sales person (in some cases "warning" is the appropriate term) about a client. Although some insights can be valuable, be aware that other's predictions about how a home buyer will behave often prove inaccurate. Clients can show an entirely new side of themselves to a new personality or under different circumstances.

Factual information is usually more helpful than predictions. If the home buyers are moving here from England, just celebrated their 25th anniversary, are both starting new jobs, or have a youngster in a wheel chair, you should be aware of these details. Similarly, know the latest about the delivery of their back-ordered chandelier or the status of the fence installation schedule. This behind-the-scenes transfer of information makes the company look attentive and in control of details.

Price and Experience

You can not predict a client's behavior on facts such as how many homes they have purchased or how much money they are spending. The first-time purchasers of an economical one-bedroom condo might be difficult, while the experienced buyer of an $800,000 six-bedroom custom home can be a delight. The reverse is equally true. Buyers' expectations and behaviors are a blend of their consumer experience, education, and ego—often defying prediction or stereotypes. However, logic and history suggest some guidelines that are worth mentioning.

First-Time Buyers. To first-time buyers, every part of this process is unfamiliar. They may have many questions but be hesitant about asking them. They may seek guidance from friends, parents, an attorney, or a hired home inspector. Such behavior may show the home buyers' lack of self-confidence, and builders should avoid taking it as an insult. Help these clients feel comfortable and welcome any questions. To earn their trust, provide accurate answers, keep them updated, and volunteer information regarding their responsibilities.

Experienced Buyers. Seasoned home buyers are familiar with the basics and may nod knowingly halfway through your explanations. The vocabulary of the home building process is less of a foreign language to these clients so communication is usually a bit easier and faster.

One danger, however, is the inevitable comparison of the current purchase to those of the past. They may believe only the methods and materials with which they are familiar are correct. Also, no two builders follow exactly the same procedures. Assuming that because these home buyers have been through this process before they need less information does a disservice to the clients and your company.

Victims of Negative Experience. Perhaps the most challenging of all home buyers are those who have had a bad experience—either a home that did not hold up well or a builder who left items incomplete. Admittedly, some negative memories may be the result of the client's inappropriate choices or unrealistic expectations. The exact source of the negative experience is less important than that the fact this home buyer will be skeptical. Careful listening and regular communication can create a sharp contrast between the bad experience of the past and the good one your company provides.

Whether you work with first-time home buyers or veterans, take nothing for granted, least of all the fragile goodwill of the anxious, excited, stressed home buyers. Caught off guard by some information or event, many clients quickly become frustrated and upset.

Home buyers don't like surprises. Anticipate and eliminate obstacles. Provide guidance and information. In short, do everything you can to help your home buyers remain comfortable. They all want the same thing in the end—a home buying experience that makes them feel good. Arrive at each meeting with an open mind, well-prepared and ready for anything. Your objective is to use information and communication to help home buyers enjoy the process and love the result.

Product Familiarity

If the floor plan involved is one with which you are unfamiliar—perhaps no showhome of that plan exists—review the floor plans and specifications, and visit the home early enough to become familiar with it. You would not want to say "Let's take a look in the basement next" as you open the guest closet. If a showhome exists and you have not visited it in a while, now is a good time to refresh your memory.

Paperwork

In preparing the paperwork for any client meeting, remember that appearing organized shows clients the skills they know are essential to building a quality home. Double check that names and addresses are correct, forms are in the proper order, and any copies you will deliver to the clients are ready to hand over. In addition to the specific paperwork needed for the meeting, bring your homeowner manual, some extra business cards, and a notepad.

Conduct

As you conduct client meetings, your research pays off and you see the impact of the knowledge and confidence you have gained. The following hints add polish and prevent problems:

- Be early for every client meeting. Be in control by welcoming the clients as they arrive.
- Begin each meeting by thanking the clients for taking time to meet with you.
- Introduce each meeting by briefly reviewing its purposes in one or two sentences. Show the client the homeowner manual entry that describes the meeting so they know where to begin in that material.
- Cover each agenda item thoroughly, answer client questions, and note any details about commitments or issues that will require follow up.
- If some unique issue arises, think and research before committing to an answer. Note the items and say "That's a good question (or important point). Let me research that and I'll get back to you <a definite day and time>."
- Avoid becoming trapped in "what if" conversations; you do not have enough information to suggest possible resolutions. Any guess you might make can haunt you later.
- As the meeting comes to a close, pause to check the agenda, confirming that you have discussed each topic.
- Review the notes you took and, as needed, explain to the clients when they can expect an update on outstanding issues. If the clients are responsible for some detail (such as a final decision on cabinet style), get their commitment for completion of that task.
- Conclude each meeting by aligning the home buyers' expectations for the next regular meeting and explain how they should handle any questions that arise in the mean time.

You will also find many specific hints and suggestions under the Parts entitled "Predictable Situations."

Follow Through

Many perform the first three steps well—schedule, prepare, and conduct—then fail to follow through. This lack of final attention can destroy the good results of all earlier work. Make tenacious and documented follow through one of the hallmarks of your work. Follow through leads to closure. Closure means that every issue raised in any client meeting has been taken care of: you know it, the client knows it, and the file proves it.

Documentation is critical to preventing misunderstanding or conflict. Should a conflict occur, documentation may resolve it, and ultimately, can be critical to your company's defense. Perhaps most important, follow through is how you provide the kind of detailed attention that delights clients and prevents problems in the first place.

7

Attitudes, Communication Skills, and Habits That Help
Act as If You Like Your Clients

This fundamental attitude—composed of such things as appreciation, respect, compassion, tolerance, enthusiasm, and resilience—will not only serve your clients well, but will help you enjoy your work.

At the same time that you like your clients, strive for true professionalism in every task. Dictionaries define professionals with phrases such has "an individual who is an expert in his or her work." In the business world, the word refers to those fantastic elusive qualities and behaviors that impress clients and command respect from peers.

Professionalism applies to any type of work. The term is difficult to define without listing examples of how it appears in behavior and performance. Professionals are not perfect, but they accept responsibility for their actions, and they have good recovery skills. Born of a passion for excellence and ever-growing competence, professionalism comes from and results in joy in one's work. Keep the following characteristics and skills in mind.

Accountability

Mistakes occur in the construction of new homes. Pretending that your company's performance is perfect, glossing over errors, making excuses, or rationalizing omissions can destroy client trust. On the other hand, showing that you will correct mistakes instills confidence with your home buyers. This applies equally to items your client may not notice. Correcting items you know are incorrect—whether the home buyers point them out—demonstrates your integrity. Ironically, this straightforward approach makes it easier for you to deny attention to items that are correct when clients want you to meet standards higher than your company promised.

Body Language

We frequently send messages without realizing it with silent communicators such as our posture, facial expression, tone of voice, gestures, and eye contact. According to linguists who have studied face-to-face communication, nonverbal elements make up as much as

78% of what a listener receives from a conversation. Knowledge of body language can help you reinforce the correct message. In addition, this insight helps you better understand the body language of a client.

Besides communicating attitude, your body language conveys your professional stature and self-confidence. Speaking with conviction in a calm voice shows clients you are confident and competent. They are more likely to trust what you say. The same holds true for colleagues, your boss, and your personal life.

Body language is a complex topic. Many excellent resources are available that address it. Until you have the opportunity to make a detailed study, keep these general points in mind.

Eye Contact

Make eye contact by looking at your clients' eyes until you know they know you looked at their eyes. Staring holes into someone is uncomfortable, and some people even consider it hostile. Yet, looking off to one side suggests someone more interesting just came into the room and can make your client wonder whether you are paying attention. Break eye contact occasionally by looking down—usually at some paperwork having to do with the clients. If you are working with a client from another culture, take your cue as to how much eye contact is appropriate from the client and demonstrate respect for his or her background.

Smiling

Show your clients that you enjoy your work and are enthusiastic about helping them by smiling at appropriate times. If you smile even when you are not feeling your best, your brain does not know the difference; it thinks you are happy. You might cheer yourself up.

Gestures

Good communication occurs when people are open with each other; reflect this attitude with your gestures. The manner in which you gesture, especially in tense conversations, can mean the difference between sending a message of trust and cooperation or hostility and defensiveness. Placing your hands on your hips conveys annoyance. Exhaling in a heavy, forceful way does the same. Folding your arms across your chest suggests distrust.

At meetings, avoid crossing your legs when you want to reinforce trust and cooperation. A relaxed but alert position works more effectively. Sit or stand asymmetrically. Keep your arms open. Be aware, too, of how you handle your briefcase, the blueprints, clipboard, or other items. Slamming something down abruptly can suggest you are angry.

Posture

Slouching and leaning can send the wrong message: I'm tired, bored, or uninterested in you and your home. At the other extreme, a too rigid posture can make you appear unfriendly. An alert and interested attitude is reinforced by a posture that is relaxed and involved. Lean forward into the conversation a bit. Let your gestures reinforce this involved image.

Tone of Voice

Your tone of voice can be interested and caring, aggressive, or submissive. Interested and caring works best for most client situations. Notice the tones of voice of others with whom you speak and your reactions to them. Pay attention to your tone of voice and be certain it conveys the attitude you want. This is especially important on the phone when visual clues are missing from the conversation. Sarcastic or harsh tones can hurt or anger clients. Sincerity and responsiveness are the messages you want to send.

Judgment Calls

As much as builders would like to have clear-cut policies and procedures that provide predictable answers to client situations, the reality is that working with home buyers is a task loaded with contradictions, exceptions, and paradoxes. Common sense and good judgment are essential.

Most builders fully intend to do the "right thing" for their clients. Sometimes, however, knowing what that "right thing" is can be difficult. Restrain your emotions, look at all sources of information, and make conscious judgment calls. You may be called upon to make judgment calls at any of three levels: physical, circumstantial, or image.

Physical Judgment: The Documents and the House

Physical judgments are usually the easiest and most comfortable. Terms of the purchase agreement or the limited warranty often provide clear answers. Comparing physical conditions to measurable standards creates confidence—a quarter of an inch last week is the same as a quarter of an inch this week.

If your conclusion is that the requested attention is not justified based on the physical evidence, you may still face two more levels of judgment. Standards are much less defined for circumstantial and image judgment.

Circumstantial Judgment: The Client's Side of the Story

No matter how much documentation builders create, circumstances occur. Paperwork and measurable criteria may not address these circumstances. Indeed, in fairness to homeowners, policies, procedures, and standards should be looked upon as merely the starting point in making customer decisions. When dealing with circumstantial decisions, keep these points in mind.

Objectivity. Avoid decisions based your personal opinion of the home buyer.

Listening. Give a fair hearing to the client's point of view. "What was it in our information that made you expect . . . ?" is an excellent question. If the client can point to something in the purchase documents, the decision may be obvious (and revising the documents may be appropriate).

Research. Back up good listening habits with research. By checking the documents and the showhome, and by talking to sales, design, construction, or trade personnel, you may uncover facts essential to a fair response.

Common Sense. Last of all, use common sense to arrive at a fair answer.

Circumstantial judgments—sifting facts from rationalizations to arrive at that "right" answer—is almost always tougher than making physical judgments. Yet, even circumstantial judgment does not generate the consternation of the third level—image judgment.

Image Judgment—Reputation at Risk

Science, properties of materials, codes, scopes of work, showhomes, purchase agreements, and warranty standards notwithstanding, clients' emotional reactions and threats can transform what was up until this point a logical process into a trip down the White Rabbit's hole. When you least expect, you might feel like Alice talking with the Madd Hatter, aka—the Madd Home Buyer. This third level of judgment is the most complex and the toughest to master.

Assume that after you inspect the home, review the documents, and listen carefully to the client's explanation of the circumstances, you conclude the correct answer to the requested attention is "no." However, the client's personality makes it clear that "no" will be the wrong answer. You now face a level three or image level judgment. If you say "no," one or more of several events, all unpleasant, can follow.

Low Survey Scores. Many builders pay bonuses for achieving a specified level of client satisfaction. Some employees may feel this income is threatened (along with their jobs) if they do not satisfy every demand of every client.

Negative Word-of-Mouth. This, of course, can result in loss of future sales.

Going Over Your Head. The client, hoping for a different answer, complains to a higher company authority.

Revenge Lists. Denied one or more items, some home buyers may get even with lengthy, nitpicky lists of questions or items they do not really care about. They want to cause extra work and expense because they are angry.

Complaints to Sales. Usually this type of tirade occurs in front of several prospective home buyers. Besides lost sales, this can cause friction between sales people and other staff members.

Instigating. Some home buyers use the "in unity there is strength" approach and lobby their neighbors to negativity. Ironically, many of these neighbors did not even know they were unhappy.

Drama. This can include picketers, signs in the yard, banners on the garage: "Before you buy here, talk to me." These clients are so angry they are willing to sacrifice the value of their property (and that of their neighbors) to hurt their builder.

Media. Negative stories sell papers and increase ratings. Once a situation is written in a newspaper, discussed on the radio, or televised, it takes on a (mostly negative) life of its own, frequently drawing support from other previously contented or neutral homeowners.

Consumer Protection Entities. Whether complaints go to a Better Business Bureau, a state licensing board, or an attorney general's office, builders must defend themselves. This costs time, money, and emotional energy.

Arbitration. While usually faster and less expensive than full blown litigation, time, money, and emotional energy must be invested.

Litigation. Playing the lawsuit lottery has become a hobby for some consumers. Even when the builder wins, the builder loses. The attention is negative, legal fees are seldom recovered, and the stress is serious.

At this point you may be tempted to provide the requested attention to avoid such potential events. Consider another set of repercussions. If you say "yes" when the real answer is "no," any or all of the following may result.

Precedent. Actually, two precedents are set. The first is with this client who learns that a well-timed threat produces the desired result; the builder's rules can be overpowered by a strong personality. The second is with the client's neighbors who hear of the incident and use similar behaviors to demand similar concessions.

Budget. Adjustments or corrections that are free to the builder will usually be approved at the physical judgment level. Beyond these, the builder can expect to write a check.

Complaints. Workloads for the company personnel and trades increase with unjustified work. They may resent the need to have contact with a hostile client.

Delays. Other clients, with justified requests, wait for attention they deserve while the squeaky wheel gets oiled.

Self-Esteem. After many of these encounters, front-line personnel may lose confidence, enjoy their work less, and suffer increased stress. They are likely to develop a cynical attitude that is conveyed to home buyers with a less enthusiastic tone of voice, slower responses, and harsher judgments. Such employees are often said to be "burned out." This leads to turnover, which is costly and disrupts service and productivity.

The knowledge and insights you gain working through the "Knowledge Is Power" Part of this Guide will help you will all levels of judgment. Especially in level three (image) situations, do not hesitate to discuss the issues with others in your company or even in the home building industry. A fresh perspective on the situation may produce an acceptable solution and add to your understanding of company philosophies—making the next issue easier for you to resolve.

Listening

Clients appreciate someone who pays attention to them. That means listening with focus and concentration, as if this home and these home buyers are important. Learn to use your body language skills to reinforce the message that you are paying attention. As with smiling, going through the motions helps you develop the corresponding attitude.

Listen with more than your ears. Listen with your eyes, using good eye contact. Add alert posture, gestures, and expressions that show you are involved. Allow a few minutes to chat casually a bit. Ask questions about the buyers' family, work, hobbies, and so on. Listening to the answers will help you understand your clients.

Avoid doing two things at once. Listening is a full-time job. Discipline yourself to focus on what the client is saying rather than using the time to think of your response. Pausing to reflect and gather your thoughts before speaking actually shows the client you are giving the matter careful consideration.

Saying No

Much as we would like to do everything any client requests, physical realities, codes, budgets, weather, and the need to achieve profitability sometimes require saying no to a client request. When this is necessary, saying no skillfully can prevent the question from escalating into a conflict. Well handled, the client can come away from the conversation respecting you and accepting your response. Two important techniques help to achieve this: the soft no and the terminal no.

Soft No

When you use the soft no, you say no without using the word no. Tell the home buyer what your company does or what is true instead of what is not. For instance "We usually handle that by . . . ." "What we do is . . . ." or "That would be a home maintenance item."

During an orientation, one buyer asked if they got a cover on an egress window well like the one on the other side of the home. The orientation rep answered "No, we don't give you those unless the window well is within 4 feet of a door." A better response would have eliminated the "no" and "don't"—"We install covers when the window well is within 4 feet of a door. If you would like a cover for this window also, you can purchase another one at . . . ."

Terminal No

Occasionally, a buyer refuses to accept a soft no, and you will need to be firmer in your response. For such occasions, use the terminal no technique. With a terminal no, you list reasons first and put the word no at the end of the answer. "Because of a and b, I must tell you no."

This is more effective than saying "No, because" followed by a list of reasons. When you say no, the person to whom you are speaking is likely to stop listening to you to consider how to change your mind. He or she therefore does not hear your reasons, which may be brilliant and convincing.

For instance, regarding a minor crack in a concrete drive, a warranty rep used the terminal no. "Concrete cracks are caused by shrinkage, soil movement, and temperature changes. These are all things outside our control and therefore are excluded from the repairs we provide. Therefore I must tell you no, we will not replace your drive."

Although the terminal no technique does not guarantee that your home buyers will like the answer or even agree with your reasons, you still have a better chance if they at least hear those reasons.

Service Maturity

If you take remarks home buyers make personally, you may lose control of your temper and lash back. This is inappropriate and generally makes things worse. The gratification of "letting someone have it" is short lived (I know this from experience). Practice service maturity—the ability to be friendly and courteous to people who are being pushy and rude.

Take into account the emotions that are involved in the new home experience and be patient when home buyers are difficult. Their frazzled nerves can magnify minor details. The most easy-going person may react disproportionately to events because of the stress—

emotional highs and lows, the number of decisions to make, endless financial details, and the regular doses (and overdoses) of adrenaline.

Forgive clients' occasional emotional outbursts and start fresh with each new contact. Caring professionals can guide the most nervous buyers through the various stages of the purchase and happily into their new homes.

When Things Go Wrong

Most of the time the documentation required for client meetings will be the meeting agenda and the notes you take during the meeting. However, in some cases, additional documentation may be appropriate, even essential. Oftentimes, when hearing an employee speak of something that happened with a client, a manager might say "Document that for the file, will you?"

Yet most companies do not provide a format or any training on what, exactly, that documentation should include or what form it should take. If your company has an established format specifically for this purpose, follow that. If not, get in the habit of using the Incident Report in Figure 7.1 for those times when you need to "document that for the file."

Completing an incident report would be appropriate after a disagreement between yourself and a client. You might observe an incident involving a trade employee or some natural disaster. Whatever the situation, complete the report while your memory is fresh. Review it the next day to check for accuracy and completeness. Confirm that you avoided inappropriate editorializing or emotional outbursts of your own. You may also find upon reflection that some improvement in your approach might have prevented the episode. If so, learn from the experience.

FIGURE 7.1 Incident Report

Date of Incident	Time
Location	
Participants	Witnesses
Events	
Signature	Date

8

Predictable Situations

Anticipating every problematic situation that could ever occur with clients is inconceivable, but by discussing some of the more obvious possibilities, you increase confidence. Rehearsing uncomfortable scenarios reduces the chances that an unusual occurrence will throw you into a panic. Consider the tough situations described here—which have occurred dozens, if not hundreds, of times.

Abusive Clients

No employee should be expected to tolerate verbal abuse, whether in the form of threats, foul language, or other intimidation techniques. Calmly end the conversation by saying something along the lines of "Mrs. Jones, I understand that you are upset. I'd like to work with you to find a solution. However, I am going to put some boundaries on how we communicate with each other. If you can stop using that kind of language, I'll continue to talk with you. Otherwise, we will end this conversation and I'll call you tomorrow to discuss this further."

If the abusive behavior continues, calmly leave the meeting or hang up the phone. Complete an incident report for the file. Mark your calendar for the follow-up call and make sure to place that call. The fact that you said you would do this makes it easier for you to initiate contact. You will often hear an apology, and in most cases, the client's future behaviors will be appropriate and businesslike—at least with you.

Baiting

When a client baits you, he or she uses your words or actions to trap you into giving the answer the client wants to hear. For example, "You people advertise that customer satisfaction is so important, let's see you back it up." Or "In a home of this price, a rear deck should be included." The key to responding is recognizing you are being baited.

When responding to baiting, keep in mind that two things can be true. Use "and" rather than "but." In response to the examples given, a good answer might be "Yes, customer satisfaction is a priority for our company and this is home maintenance." Or "Yes, customer satisfaction is a priority for our company and adding a deck to your home plans will increase the price."

Another version of the baiting technique is appealing to your personal standards. The implication is that you and the client share the same high standards: "Would you accept this in your home?" If you say "No, I would not" you'll have a hard time refusing to repair or replace the item in question. If you say "Yes, I'd accept this" you are, according to the client's logic, saying that you have low standards—something no professional would want to do. It seems no reasonable response exists. However, you can acknowledge "This is less than perfect and if I got the rest of the home with it, I'd accept it."

Buyers Disagree with Each Other

When partners in a purchase are unable to agree on design, financial priorities, timing issues, or any other aspect of the transaction, your safest course is to stay out of the way. Attempts at counseling are likely to alienate one or both of your home buyers. Instead of taking sides, provide the facts, describe their options and the pros and cons of each, set a clear deadline for their final decision, and give them private time to talk through the issues.

Buyers Misquote or Misunderstand

Anyone can misunderstand a conversation. Memories are imperfect tools, and the passage of time weakens them further. This is one of the main reasons that detailed documentation is so useful. However, when you encounter a consistent pattern of clients misquoting you, something is amiss. First, check yourself. Do you explain details clearly and in logical order? Do you answer questions completely and accurately? Sometimes what seemed completely clear to you when you said it is heard differently by clients, and may be recalled in another version later.

Avoid construction jargon that might confuse folks unfamiliar with it. Practice your explanations on family or friends until you know you are communicating clearly. When you encounter a client who has a lot of questions, discuss details and confirm the client understands what you have said.

If a client misquotes or misunderstands some information, it may be due to poor listening skills, stress, language barriers, and so on. If you work with a client under any of these circumstances, invest the time and effort to confirm that the home buyer understands each point (see "Language Barrier"). If the client consistently twists memories of conversations in the client's favor, you might be dealing with a dishonest client (see "Dishonest Client"), and special effort is required to prevent further problems.

Dishonest Client

Rare, but possible, a client may be less than trustworthy. A small percentage of clients might try to manipulate or lie to coerce you into providing extras, refunds, reductions in price, and other concessions. When you suspect that you are working with such a character, take precautions to protect yourself and your company. These might include the following techniques:

- Schedule two people from your company for all meetings with clients whose integrity is questionable, ideally a man and a woman should attend all such meetings. Each gender will recall different details, and together, they offer a more complete view of what occurred. Having two company representatives provides two witnesses to what occurred.

- Document every detail, including all issues discussed and the decisions made on each: Who will be responsible for taking action? What action? By what deadline? Who pays the cost?

- Take time to think through your responses to any routine questions. Remember that shoot-from-the-hip answers cause problems. "That's an important issue. Let me investigate the details and I'll get back to you <date and time>."

- Be cautious about changing well-established policies or long-standing documents. Problems often develop when builders venture into unfamiliar territory solely because a client is insistent.

- Respond promptly and in writing with well-researched and carefully worded answers. These should be technically correct, legally appropriate, and diplomatically, but clearly phrased. Avoid getting even with sarcasm, volleying accusations, or hurling insults.

- Establish a relationship with an attorney (or attorneys) experienced in residential construction and contract issues. Contact this person sooner rather than later to discuss the situation and obtain guidance.

- Network with other professionals in your region and those you meet at conferences and conventions.

- Avoid allowing a bad client to make you cynical. Maintain a healthy perspective; most clients are fair-minded, reasonable people who just want a new home.

- Learn from your experiences, fine-tune your paperwork and processing systems, and continue improving your skills.

Emergencies

Examples of emergencies include someone getting injured or becoming ill, or smelling the odor of natural gas in a client home, or discovering a home has been vandalized. In any emergency, your first priority is to protect the people involved. Get all parties to a safe location and call for appropriate emergency help. Once the people are safe, the property is your next concern. Again, call the appropriate authorities. As soon as possible, complete an incident report (Figure 7.1)

Gender Bias

Gender bias occurs when we treat one person differently from another because of his or her gender. This customer relations error is caused by stereotyping the sexes or making assumptions. For instance, many builders have created ill-will with the woman of the household by directing discussion of construction to the man of the household. Others have created problems by directing all their remarks to an outgoing woman and ignored a man who was quiet and reserved. Avoid all versions of gender bias by using eye contact and gestures to keep both parties involved in the discussion. Listen to what they both have to say without interrupting, and answer all questions completely, speaking in a respectful tone.

Going Over Your Head

When a home buyer does not like your answer, he or she may appeal to a higher authority in the hope of obtaining a different response. Keep in mind that the client would take this step even if you and the higher authority traded places. The solution is training the higher authority in how to respond. This company owner, vice president, or department head should take the following steps:

- Listen to the client, take notes.
- Thank the client for bringing the situation to the company's attention.
- Commit to a review of all facts and circumstances.
- Promise an update within a stated time frame (24–72 hours, in most cases).
- Contact you to discuss the situation.
- Get the history of the situation.
- Review available options.
- Did you let this get personal? Often with a difficult client, the tendency to go "by-the-book" is strong and can get in the way of common sense exceptions.
- Do external circumstances make keeping peaceful relations essential? If your company is about to request re-zoning of a parcel of land, the last thing it needs is an angry client who is picketing at the site. Such conditions influence the decisions of the higher authority—as they would you, if roles were reversed (see "Judgment Calls").
- Involve you in any meetings or inspections with the homeowner (unless doing so would escalate the situation further).
- If the final decision is to repeat the denial, the higher authority should deliver the answer. Should your discussion discover some fact you overlooked, or if circumstances suggest changing the answer to a yes, you should deliver that answer and oversee the adjustment.

Objectivity often slips away when you feel you are under attack in these situations. Once individuals—yourself included—have taken a position, backing down can be uncomfortable. If your communication with the home buyer has been courteous, reversing your original answer will be easier. "Mrs. Jones, given the information I have at this point, my answer is no. Is there anything you think I've overlooked?"

Likewise, work to provide your client with a way to back down from a position he or she has taken. "I can understand why you might think that, however, you may not be aware that. . . ." or " I once thought that too. Then I learned . . . and I changed my mind." By offering the home buyer a graceful way out, you may prevent the "going over my head" behavior altogether.

Good Cop, Bad Cop

"This doesn't bother me, but my husband/wife/partner is likely to become hysterical if you don't take care of it." When one partner represents that the other is upset, angry, or adamant about something and that other partner is not present, you may wonder who really wants what.

After a roof leak damaged the drywall, a warranty rep worked on cosmetic repairs three times for a woman who claimed her husband was dissatisfied with the quality of the repair.

When the warranty rep saw the husband in a local restaurant and mentioned the work, it turned out that the woman's husband had been out of town and did not even know the roof had leaked.

When an absent party's opinion is used to get more attention, try to get everyone together to review the situation and agree on a final resolution. As in any client situation, document each detail of the resolution and follow through carefully.

Home Improvement Store Syndrome

The 2001 edition of the *Homeowner Manual Template,* published by Home Builder Press, contains this entry in the Part entitled "Construction of Your Home":

Single Source

[Builder] is a single source company. That means that we select all personnel and companies who will contribute to your home. We order all materials and products from suppliers with whom we have established relationships. Although sweat equity arrangements are unavailable as a part of our purchase agreement, you are welcome to add your personal touches to the home after you close and take possession of it.

In many cases, the best approach to heading off difficulties with clients is to get to the topic first—or at least be prepared for the client to mention the subject. This applies to many aspects of the home building process, as you will see throughout this Guide. When a client says, "I found the jetted bathtub I want at <home improvement warehouse> cheaper than you can get it" you need to be ready to respond.

"Clients often ask us about purchasing materials themselves. Our experience has led us to a commitment to be a single source company. Let me explain why. . . ." Go on to provide a couple of examples of the problems that arise from working this way, concluding that "[Builder] is therefore a single source company. You are welcome to add whatever you like to the home after you close on it. We order, install, and are responsible for everything up to that point."

If your company determines that it makes good business sense to allow sweat equity arrangements with home buyers, be certain a written agreement clearly defines responsibilities.

I'll Be Glad to Find Out

Although you can easily find a couple of people who believe otherwise, no one in the home building industry knows everything about home building. You have no reason to feel embarrassed because you cannot answer every question a client asks. When you do not know, admit it by saying something such as "I'll be glad to research that" "Let's ask about that" or "I'll find out for you."

If you pretend you know when you do not or attempt to cover your ignorance by changing the subject, the client may sense this and lose respect for you. Be honest, take good notes about open issues, and follow up meticulously. Each time you research something for a client, you serve that client and expand your knowledge for next time.

Interruptions: Phones, Pagers, or People

The buzzing, beeping, or ringing of any phone, pager, or radio you carry interrupts conversations and may suggest to home buyers that other matters are more important to you. During any scheduled meeting with a client, turn all of your electronic leashes off. Two exceptions exist. One is when you are waiting for someone to provide information related to that client's home. The second is when you expect some urgent news, such as your wife has gone into labor. Explain the reason you are leaving your phone on to the client. Keep all subsequent phone or radio conversations as short as possible.

Trades people and other company staff should recognize that when you are with a client, interruptions for anything but emergencies should wait until you are free. If someone unfamiliar with your position on this interrupts your client conversation, simply say "I'll be happy to talk with you when I'm finished working with Mr. and Mrs. Jones" and return to your clients. Later, explain the policy to the person who interrupted to prevent a recurrence.

Inventory Sale

When the home you sold already exists, your clients have less input and less opportunity to trust your company. Because most of the activities discussed in the first two client meetings (preconstruction conference and frame stage tour) are already complete, you might think the buyers do not need to hear the information. However, schedule an abbreviated session that lasts 30 to 45 minutes; walk through other sites or homes under construction to point out quality techniques and features to the clients. This attention also makes the home buyers feel important.

Language Barriers

Demographic reports and daily experience tell us that the number of clients from other cultures who are purchasing homes is increasing dramatically. Although we appreciate the business, some challenges accompany these sales. Difficulty communicating due to language differences is an obvious one.

Short of refusing to sell to someone who does not speak English, what can you do? Learning some of the language—if one culture is prevalent in your region—might offer you some relief, and such efforts are appreciated by foreign clients. Find and create business relationships with reliable interpreters (another employee, a professional interpreter, or a translating service). When working directly with a home buyer whose ability to speak English is still improving, keep this hints in mind:

- Speak slowly, using short sentences. Your client must translate your remark into his or her language, consider your comment, respond to it, and then translate the response into English to say it to you. This takes a bit of time, and long remarks from you will cause confusion.
- Avoid speaking louder. The fact that clients do not speak English does not mean they are deaf.
- Avoid slang, jargon, and blended phrases such as "Whatcha up to?"

■ Follow normal company procedures and standards—subject to common sense. Avoid setting the precedent of allowing a client dictate terms because explaining normal policies wears you out.

Left-Out Spouse

A spouse or partner can be left out of the new home process physically or emotionally, or can be left out of the communications. The appropriate response to all of these conditions begins with recognizing what is happening. Once you notice that someone is left-out, make a special effort to involve the left-out partner. This extra initial work will ultimately save you time.

Physical

One partner may be physically left out because the former home needs to be sold, the children need to complete the school year, or the new baby needs to be born before the final move can take place. When you meet or talk to the second partner, send greetings and ask if the other partner has any questions. Call the left-out partner occasionally with updates; send some photos or a short note. When the missing partner arrives, offer to repeat the most recent meeting—in an abbreviated version—and review information already provided to the involved partner. This is especially important in the case of the orientation.

Emotional

Sometimes because of a job transfer or other circumstances, families move even though one partner would prefer to remain in the former location. You cannot correct this. However, you can communicate often and in a friendly and helpful manner. Avoid creating an informational void that might make the left-out partner feel more negative. Try to understand the cause for the lack of enthusiasm and have empathy for the person. Correct any issues according to normal company standards and policies.

Communication

Occasionally you will work with clients who do not communicate well between themselves. This can be a sign that they are extremely busy, or it can signal serious problems in their relationship. Whatever the cause, you may hear complaints from one of the partners that you have not provided information or attention as promised. Avoid any remark that suggests you believe their relationship is not a good one or that the responsibility for sharing information is theirs. Simply say "I apologize for not updating you. The change order has been approved and all we need is your signature and payment." In the future, work to keep both parties updated.

Although all of these efforts create more work, they save time because you seldom need to defend yourself and have fewer problems with clients who are comfortable, involved, and informed.

Let's Make a Deal

You may encounter clients who ask for financial compensation for a disappointment or inconvenience they experience during the relationship. A client may offer to "let go" of one concern in exchange for something else—a check, an upgrade, a tree, or so forth.

Strive to achieve consistent performance and quality in all our homes and processes. If something is wrong, fix that something. Keep the resolution within the category of the error. If the problem involves concrete, repair the concrete. A complaint about concrete should not be resolved by providing a garage door opener. To do so creates three potential future problems.

First, others who visit the home and see the bad concrete work may assume that is the typical quality of the company. Second, after clients discover that this tactic works, they search high and low for other errors to use as bargaining points. And third, if the original homeowner sells the home, the second owner may re-open the issue.

If some circumstances evolve that make you feel a token of appreciation for your client is appropriate, by all means provide one. For example, when a builder in Florida had a difficult time correcting a roof leak, the homeowners were patient and kept a sense of humor. When the problem was finally cured, the builder sent them a gift certificate for dinner to a popular restaurant. Such gifts should be your idea and are certainly appropriate when circumstances merit.

Out-of-State Buyers

When your home buyers live out of state and are unavailable for any or all of the normal meetings, make a special effort to help them feel involved. Regular reports by fax, phone, or mail, perhaps with an occasional photo or even a video tape can build a relationship at the same time you build the home. The time invested pays off later with goodwill and a buyer comfort level not attainable without such attention.

Personality Conflict

No one expects that every client will be your favorite home buyer. When you work with a large number of people, personality conflicts are possible. Cultivate unflappable courtesy and an ability to work with a variety of personalities and communication styles.

When you encounter friction, identify the differences between your two personalities. Discover what you can emphasize more to get along with this home buyer. For example, engineers are notoriously detail oriented. Make a special effort to respond to this home buyer with precision and thoroughness.

Take pride in being tolerant of diverse personalities and in your ability to work with them. If a situation becomes unmanageable, consider whether you might get another staff member to take over for you (see "Service Maturity").

Scheduling Issues

Almost everyone has too many things on their to-do lists. Combine this with the challenges of arriving on time despite traffic congestion, and schedules become a real challenge. For those working with home buyers, this challenge takes several forms.

Buyers Are Late

How long should you wait? Twenty minutes is a common guideline. The individual who set the appointment should call the home buyers to discover what went wrong. In some cases, you will be able to adjust your schedule, and start the meeting late. If this does not work, offer to reschedule rather than rush a meeting. When you hurry, important details can be overlooked; confusion can result, and you open the door to someone saying "We had to hurry at our <meeting> so that's why you owe us something more now."

Buyers Are Unavailable

If your clients live so far from their new home that attending meetings is impractical, avoid concluding that you can skip the meeting entirely. Instead, look for another method besides a face-to-face gathering. Use conference calls, videos, or photos to cover the usual agenda as closely as possible.

Buyers Insist on Off-Hours Appointments

By thinking through scheduling issues and describing the parameters of available appointments in your homeowner manual, you will prevent most disagreement with clients about scheduling. Sales people help significantly by mentioning to clients that building a new home is an investment of money, emotion, and time.

When a client says "I need an appointment in the evening" rather than responding, "No, that's not possible," answer "Appointments are available Monday through Friday between 8:00 a.m. and 3:00 p.m."

Some companies are able to offer appointments on Saturdays. If company personnel can conduct meetings effectively and maintain that schedule until the subdivision is complete, this may provide the flexibility needed. Be certain the offer can be sustained without damaging morale or disrupting other essential duties.

Silence Is Golden

Sometimes the best thing to say is nothing. Often a home buyer will think out loud or make an observation that needs no response other than an acknowledgment that you heard it. Imagine that during an orientation a client says, "I've noticed it takes longer for the hot water to get to the master bath than it does the hall bath." Your response is "Yes, sir, it does" followed by silence.

To continue with an explanation, that the water heater is further away from the master bedroom, might lead to the home buyer asking why the water heater was not centered. You could then say "Probably because we wanted all the utilities at one end of the basement in case you decide to finish it." And now your home buyer says "It's not important to me to finish the basement. Fast hot water is my priority. I want the tank moved." Things go down hill from here.

Television and the Internet

As with the home improvement store syndrome, being prepared for "I was watching an episode of "Homes R Us" last Saturday and I saw. . ." makes responding much easier and less likely to create conflict. Empathize with your client. You might comment "Buyers often have questions after watching such shows and that's understandable. We keep an eye on what's new in methods and materials. This is such an important issue that the subject is covered in our homeowner manual. What it says is. . . " and proceed to paraphrase your manual. Borrowing again from the 2001 edition of the *Homeowner Manual Template*, including the following paragraph in your manual helps to back up your position on this issue:

> Television and the Internet
>
> You may be aware of various home construction methods and materials from watching television programs or exploring the Internet. [Builder] routinely reviews new approaches with a focus on building homes with materials and methods that perform predictably and to our standards. While we will be happy to discuss alternative methods and materials you may be interested in, we take a conservative approach to new methods and materials until they have been proven over time. In addition, what is appropriate for a home in one area may not be appropriate for your home due to soil, climate, and other conditions.

Third Parties

To reduce the likelihood of third parties attending client meetings, explain to your home buyers that a great deal of information is covered at each meeting, and the company wants the home buyers' undivided attention. Suggest that visits to the home involving third parties—relatives, inspectors, or real estate agents—can occur at another time. Include this information in your homeowner manual, and remind the clients of it when setting the meeting appointments. Conduct each meeting in a businesslike manner, on time and according to the agenda. Accustomed to this tone, your clients are likely to approach the meetings with the same attitude.

Even though you've taken these preventive steps, some clients will arrive with extra people. No, you cannot tell them to wait in the car. Extra people at clients meetings can sometimes be helpful. A third party may act as interpreter when a language barrier exists. Third parties can reassure nervous clients that things are progressing normally. However, third parties almost always make the meetings longer because of extra conversations. They may reinforce unrealistic expectations or unreasonable demands. Third parties can have a hidden agenda or be outright hostile because of experiences they have had with another builder.

Negative experiences have conditioned many in the home building industry to dread meetings involving third parties. Rather than assume the worst, think of third parties as an opportunity to make a good impression and become another potential source of referrals. Welcome the third person courteously and include him or her in the conversation.

Your standards and procedures should remain the same. Follow them. The company does not have a second edition of the homeowner manual with extra high standards or more flexible policies, especially for third parties. Explain that your procedures and standards are subject to common sense interpretation and not open to negotiations. Show respect and courtesy for the clients' guest. Your goal is to turn the third party into a supporter, or at least deflate the hostility.

Real Estate Agent

Good relations with the real estate community are vital to the long-term success of most builders. Your company can supply information, either through short meetings or mailings, about your services and policies. Offering this information before client meetings can prevent problems. For a detailed discussion of this subject and a model for broker information, refer to *Sales Management Took Kit*, written by Dennis Radice and published by Home Builder Press.

Sometimes agents become so focused on justifying their commissions or impressing the home buyers with how aggressive they are on the buyers' behalf, they forget the original purpose: to close the existing deal. You may also be suffering because of bad experiences an agent had with another builder. Whatever the motivation, your challenge is the same—to conclude this business relationship successfully. A reminder—whether the agent is acting as a buyer's agent, seller's agent, dual agent, or transaction agent—that the real estate agent only gets paid when the deal closes can often help.

"I want to thank you for your support today. Like yourself, our goal is to get these folks into their new home, get paid for our work and get you your commission. My company appreciates the work you've done and is looking forward to selling more homes with your help."

A useful follow-up technique is to contact the agent after the closing has occurred. Ask for feedback on how your company performed in this transaction. Offer to answer any questions. Such recognition of agents' professional contribution can build rapport, making future transactions with the same agent (or others from the same brokerage) go more smoothly.

Private Home Inspector

Some customers want to hire an inspector of their own to view the home during construction or before delivery. When the buyers pay a professional home inspector, that inspector often feels pressure to find items to justify the fee. Ideally, the sales counselor is aware that the buyers intend to hire an inspector and has an opportunity to cover company policies on the subject. These can be covered in the purchase agreement, a separate document, or the homeowner manual. For example, this entry is offered by the *Homeowner Manual Template*:

Private Home Inspectors

If you wish to retain the services of a private home inspector to review your home during or at the end of construction, please be aware of [Builder] policies regarding private home inspectors. Your inspector:

- Must provide us with evidence of current worker's compensation and liability insurance.
- Should be a member of a professional association such as the American Society of Home Inspectors.

- Should be familiar with the codes applicable in your jurisdiction.
- Should be experienced with new home construction.
- Is responsible for staying informed as to the stage of construction the home has reached.
- Should avoid making any markings on the home itself.
- Should provide you and [Builder] with a written report of any concerns.
- [Builder] will address concerns involving building code or contract issues.

{Optional} Your sales counselor can provide you with a list of private home inspectors who have provided us with evidence of the required insurance as well as information about typical fees and services they offer.

If buyers present you with an inspection report, graciously accept it for review and response. Refusing to accept the report only aggravates the client who will then translate the points raised by the inspector into a verbal or written demand of their own. The issue is not the source of the items, but the condition of each of them.

Unrealistic Expectations

Some home buyers want your company's product to meet standards above those the organization advertised, contracted, or got paid for. One response to such demands is "Your standards are even higher than ours. We should deliver the product we promised. If you want to make it even better, we'll be glad to assist you with whatever information we have available."

Another possible response is to ask with a sincere tone "What was it in our communication with you that made you expect. . . ?" If the client can point to some documentation or has a good point about confusing communication, you probably owe that client some adjustment. Most often, the question helps the client realize they made an assumption.

What If . . . ?

All builder personnel should avoid participating in "What if . . . ?" conversations with clients. Speculating on such topics as what will happen to the adjacent farm land, the city's street lights, or the elementary school across the street are all dangerous. The actual events are likely to evolve in any way but the one you suggest while the client will recall your comments word for word. Avoid the "what if" trap with "I would not want to guess" or "We'll all need to wait and see."

Won't Take No for an Answer

Persistent customers may repeat requests for items despite clear responses. When this occurs, cheerfully repeat the explanation and offer assistance by way of information. This is the broken record technique—use it without losing patience. A useful response is "If something has changed or if I've overlooked something, I'll be happy to reconsider. Otherwise my original answer remains unchanged." This can keep the lines of communication open. If something has changed, you should reconsider; if not, at least you have been friendly.

Preconstruction Conference

Expectations for the Building Process

Builders who routinely conduct preconstruction conferences report dramatic differences between home buyers who take advantage of this opportunity and those who do not. If you think about how this meeting fits into the home buying experience, you'll see why this is true.

Builders sell a process as well as a home. Events that are normal in that process can alarm uninformed home buyers or erode their trust in the company. Thorough preparation supported with ongoing communication throughout construction can prevent most of this. Just as showhomes and homeowner manuals help align home buyers expectations about your product, the preconstruction conference helps align expectations about the building process.

Transfer of Trust

As mutual trust and understanding develop, home buyers usually bond with their sales person. The preconstruction conference is an opportunity to extend this trust to the construction superintendent. Confidence in the person in charge of building the new home allows home buyers to relax. The lines of communication that are established often make resolving questions easier if issues do arise. The amount of staff time invested in preconstruction conferences is returned to the company many times over in problems prevented.

Confirmation of Plans and Specifications

In a practical sense, the preconstruction conference offers everyone an opportunity to double check the accuracy of paperwork with regard to floor plans, elevations, selections, and change orders. Misunderstandings or omissions are easier to correct while they are still on paper than after they appear in the actual home during construction.

Unresolved Issues

Should any last minute worries or questions exist in the clients' minds, now is the time to draw them out. At the end of the preconstruction conference, all parties should be aligned about the home, the process of construction, and how to communicate during that process. Meeting notes document any last-minute details that require follow up as well as the ultimate resolution of those details.

Preparation Check and Balance

The preparation required for this meeting benefits the builder beyond the positive effects on the buyer relationship. In reviewing the file, superintendents discover overlooked questions or conflicting details. The comprehensive reexamination of the paperwork—such as the plans, specifications, selections, change orders, and budget—is an excellent housekeeping exercise. Now is the time to find confusing design details, unsigned change orders, unpaid options, and any other discrepancies.

Attention Invested

Finally, whether they are purchasing an affordable or a high end custom home, home buyers appreciate the attention of company personnel and enjoy talking about their new home in detail. The message that clients are important is clear. The excitement of the process contributes to the positive side of the home building experience.

9

Policies and Procedures

Preconstruction conferences are usually held after most decisions about the home are made and just before construction begins. The home buyers, sales person, and the superintendent should attend. In most companies, the sales person sets up this meeting. Coordinating the schedules of all these people can be your company's first preconstruction conference challenge.

Schedule

Depending on the company's operational style (production, semi-custom, or custom), plan on between 1 and 4 hours for preconstruction conferences. Because sales and construction should both attend, establish mutually agreed upon parameters for scheduling based on the days and times both professionals are reasonably available—blocking out times for routine staff meetings and so on.

Sales Concerns

Preconstruction conferences are often held at the sales office. If this is true in your case, one of the primary concerns of the sales people will be "How do we handle prospects who come into the sales office during a preconstruction conference?" No magic answers exist. The choices are the obvious ones:

- Offer appointments for preconstruction conferences only outside normal sales office hours. While this limits appointment times available to home buyers, those appointments will be uninterrupted.
- During preconstruction conference appointments, schedule additional coverage— perhaps a sales host or another sales person. The down sides of this approach include the hourly costs of hosting staff or the original sales person's resistance to sharing sales revenues with another sales person.

- The sales person attending the preconstruction conference might simply excuse him- or herself to work with the prospect. Some clients may be offended by such an interruption, especially if it happens more than once during their meeting. The sales person being away from part of the preconstruction conference can result in later confusion because not everyone heard everything that was said. Another concern is that the prospect may not receive the full attention of the sales person who is rushing to get back to the preconstruction conference.

Large Volume Production Concerns

Large volume companies will encounter yet another scheduling challenge. High productivity will soon have the superintendent preparing for, conducting, or following through on preconstruction conferences continuously, reducing the time available for managing the actual construction of the homes. Choices are limited.

- Although not providing as much individual attention, group preconstruction conferences can be organized. Rather than repeat information for each home buyer, sessions in which several home buyers attend a presentation together can be held; save time for individual questions at the end. Instead of having eight 2-hour meetings, the superintendent and the sales person have one 2-hour meeting and an hour of questions afterward. This more limited schedule opens the possibility of having mortgage company and design center representatives involved.
- Another option is to establish an assistant superintendent position to support field operations while the superintendent works with the home buyers. One advantage to this approach is that potential new superintendents gain field experience at the same time that home buyers get individual attention from their superintendent.
- A home buyer manager might conduct all the preconstruction conferences and then meet with the superintendent to review significant details regarding the construction of the home. This solution offers consistency but also brings the overhead of another salary and risks that important points might be missed or conveyed to the superintendent inaccurately.
- Add more superintendents to the staff so each is responsible for fewer homes, has time to meet with home buyers, and can still run job sites.

Each of these choices has advantages and disadvantages. No easy answers exist; to gain the benefits of the preconstruction conference, every company must work hard to find the procedures that fit its particular needs. The benefits are well worth the effort because satisfied clients promote the company through word-of-mouth marketing.

Each organization arrives at slightly different policies; these differ within communities and product lines. The overriding goal is to balance flexible scheduling for clients and the needs of on-site personnel to perform other duties in a reasonable manner. One caution—avoid pressuring sales people and superintendents into working around the clock; this fosters resentment, burnout, and turnover.

Preparing the Clients

When you schedule the appointment, explain to clients that the purpose, as described in their homeowner manual, is to review all plans and specifications, discuss the construction process, and answer any questions. Consider the following points:

- Provide the home buyers with a copy of the printed agenda; you might include it in your homeowner manual.
- Ensure that the home buyers have copies of related documents such as the soil report, perc test, water test, completed budget, or final specs to read ahead of time and note questions.
- Forward any remaining paper work for selected options or change requests.
- Remind the home buyers if payments are due for last-minute changes or upgrades.
- Suggest clients bring their homeowner manual with them for reference and store new paperwork from this meeting.
- If applicable, remind them that a site visit will follow the discussion in the office and suggest they dress accordingly.

Prepare

If you were building a new home, what kind of person would you have in charge of construction? Logic suggests you would want someone who:

- Knows the technical side of construction.
- Can manage the job site effectively and work well with trade contractors.
- Shows enthusiasm for the work and the end product.
- Is familiar with the plans and specifications of the home.
- Listens carefully and makes good suggestions to achieve desired goals.
- Is well-organized and on top of the details.
- Uses common sense and a problem-solving mind set.
- Communicates well and is responsive to questions.
- Shows empathy to emotional home buyers.

Clearly these traits are not demonstrated by someone who arrives late, drops the blue prints on the way into the meeting, has the wrong selection sheets, forgot to bring business cards or something to write with, lost a change order, answers three unrelated calls during the meeting, is unable to find key documents to answer questions, and misplaces the notes for follow-up tasks.

Thorough preparation and attention to detail are the keys to a successful preconstruction conference. Going into the meeting familiar with the file and ready to discuss the construction process in an orderly and authoritative manner creates client confidence and lets you enjoy the meeting. Think of your preparation for the preconstruction conference as occurring in two steps: housekeeping on the file and strategizing with the sales person.

Housekeeping

Use your preconstruction conference agenda as a checklist for assembling the needed materials. The sample agendas shown in Figures 9.1 and 9.2 include suggested preconstruction conference topics that apply to custom and production builders, respectively.

Agreed upon changes in the plans, specs, or other documents should now be complete. Confirm that you have all pages of the house plans and related detail drawings, in the most current version. Assemble all the documents in the order in which you will discuss them, with copies attached if any materials still need to be delivered to the home buyers. Tag items you need to question, documents that still need signatures or payment, or subjects you want to emphasize.

Your agenda may be different from either of the examples, but it should be printed, preferably on no carbon required (NCR) paper, so you can take notes on it during the meeting and conveniently provide the clients with an exact copy at the conclusion. Having an established agenda encourages consistency and creates documentation of the meeting at the same time.

If your company is just beginning to hold preconstruction conferences, use a single sheet agenda until you have fine tuned the topics listed on it. When the content has stabilized, order professionally printed copies. Meanwhile, be prepared to copy your meeting notes to provide the clients with a duplicate record that matches your own. Note that your clients will now expect this same procedure at the subsequent meetings. Your company literally trains the clients—creating comfort for them and an orderly process for the company.

Standard Supplies

Include your copy of the company's homeowner manual in the materials you bring to the preconstruction conference. Tag the page that describes the preconstruction conference and other entries you want to emphasize so you can turn to them quickly during the meeting.

If private home inspectors are common in your area, your standard materials for preconstruction conferences might include a copy of the building department's inspection card. This shows clients that an authority outside your company double checks the work.

Copies of home inspection reports from several inspection companies further support realistic client expectations. Use a black felt pen to mark out homeowner names and addresses. Highlight boiler plate clauses and disclaimers, such as statements that the inspector was "unable to confirm that all electrical wiring meets applicable building codes." Seeing that such remarks are routinely included in these reports to protect the inspector makes them less frightening if your home buyers read the same comment in a report on their new home.

Strategize

Visit with the sales person to learn about your home buyers' experience level and subjects of special interest or concern. If any controversial issues have come up, make certain you and the sales person provide consistent explanations and responses.

As the sales person summarizes the relationship up to this point, he or she will bring up key issues. For instance, "They've asked twice whether we can remove the dead tree from the adjacent land. I've explained we do not own that land and have no authority to take down the tree." Or "The husband is concerned about costs, and the wife wants a flat backyard for a play area. We gave them a $500 design concession, and I've reviewed their drainage plan with them twice." Being advised that "His brother is a plumber" can prevent getting caught unprepared for the request that the brother be permitted to plumb the home. The goals in this part of your preparation are to do the following:

FIGURE 9.1 Sample Preconstruction Conference Agenda: Custom

Purchaser's Address _____ Date _____

At the office:

☐ 1. Site plan

☐ 2. Soil report

☐ 3. Drainage plan

☐ 4. Status of permit

☐ 5. Utilities status

☐ 6. Status of Design Review approval

☐ 7. Other HOA issues

☐ 8. Submit landscape plans to Design Review

☐ 9. Blueprints
    a. Elevations
    b. Floor Plan
    c. Cabinet layout
    d. Mantel
    e. Electrical
    f. Other

☐ 10. Specifications

☐ 11. Selections and options

☐ 12. Timetable for remaining selections

☐ 13. Change orders

☐ 14. Change order cut-off schedule

☐ 15. Target start date

☐ 16. General construction sequence/schedule

☐ 17. Events that will extend schedule

☐ 18. "Nothing's happening"

☐ 19. Quality, builder's inspections

☐ 20. Site visit guidelines
    a. Safety
    b. Security
    c. Work in progress
    d. Something's missing

☐ 21. How to handle questions

☐ 22. Scheduled site visits

☐ 23. Draw schedule and procedures

☐ 24. Payment due at this time

☐ 25. Next payment due date

☐ 26. Target delivery date

☐ 27. Reminder: read maintenance and warranty information

☐ 28. Other [Builder] topics:

☐ 29. Other Client topics:

☐ 30. Tentative time for next meeting, to be confirmed by [Builder]

At the site:

☐ 31. Lot boundaries

☐ 32. Set backs

☐ 33. Easements

☐ 34. Orientation of home

☐ 35. Trees and other natural features

☐ 36. Drainage issues

☐ 37. Drive / culvert

☐ 38. Utility trenches

☐ 39. Construction
    a. Elevations
    a. Utilities
    b. Trash
    c. Sanitary facility

☐ 40. Mail box

Purchaser _____

Date _____

Purchaser _____

Date _____

Builder _____

Date _____

FIGURE 9.2 Sample Preconstruction Conference Agenda: Production

Purchaser's Address _____ Date _____

At the office:
- ☐ 1. Site plan
- ☐ 2. Soil report
- ☐ 3. Drainage plan
- ☐ 4. Status of permit
- ☐ 5. Utilities status
- ☐ 6. Homeowner association issues
- ☐ 7. Landscape plans
- ☐ 8. House plans
- ☐ 9. Specifications
- ☐ 10. Selections and options
- ☐ 11. Change orders
- ☐ 12. Change order cut-off schedule
- ☐ 13. Target start date
- ☐ 14. Construction sequence/schedule
- ☐ 15. Events that extend schedule
- ☐ 16. "Nothing's happening"
- ☐ 17. Quality, builder's inspection of work
- ☐ 18. Site visit guidelines
- ☐ 19. Something's missing
- ☐ 20. How to handle questions
- ☐ 21. Pre-drywall tour

- ☐ 22. Target deliver
- ☐ 23. Read maintenance and warranty
- ☐ 24. Other [Builder] topics:
- ☐ 25. Other Client topics:

At the site:
- ☐ 26. Lot boundaries and easements
- ☐ 27. Orientation of home
- ☐ 28. Trees and other natural features
- ☐ 29. Drainage
- ☐ 30. Mailbox location

Purchaser _____

Date _____

Purchaser _____

Date _____

Builder _____

Date _____

- ■ Avoid disagreements between sales and construction in front of the home buyers.
- ■ Minimize surprises that leave open issues and create unnecessary follow-up.
- ■ Eliminate the need for the home buyers to repeat their story. Be familiar with their needs and situation.

Conduct

The atmosphere at this meeting should be one of anticipation, excitement, and fun. The planning stage is at an end; the physical work is about to begin. Although a lot of information is covered, many questions answered, and significant points made, the overall mood should be one of enjoyment. Refreshments can be part of the meeting. Weather permitting, take some photographs of the buyers on the site to add to the mood of celebration.

Introduction

In addition to arriving early and setting up, take charge of the meeting and impress clients by creating a smooth transition from the sales person to you. The sales person might introduce you to the home buyers, briefly telling them something about you.

Shake hands and provide business cards. Chat for a few minutes, showing you know at least some of the facts about the clients. Be prepared with a 90-second introduction of yourself that describes your education and experience in the home building industry. Then, introduce the preconstruction conference.

"Thanks for taking the time to meet with us today. As you know we want to review the final paperwork for your new home and talk about what the building process will be like. I also want to answer any questions you have. If you refer to page 14 of your homeowner manual, you'll see where we are in our process. I like to begin with the site plan . . . ." Begin working your way through the agenda topics.

Agenda

As applicable, discuss each agenda item, including questions that you noted and any items that the clients bring up. Use the agenda as an aid to memory, without making it the center of attention.

Give the clients a chance to talk about themselves, their lifestyle, and reasons they want certain things certain ways in their new home. You may not be able to cure all of their worries and fulfill all of their dreams, but the better you understand them, the less likely you will be caught off-guard. If you encounter the occasional client obsession (such as the client who wanted the rod in his closet exactly 63.5 inches long because he counted his pants and wanted 1 inch of space between each hanger), note it to try to avoid any problems later.

Pause a couple of times to review the list quickly and catch any items that need to be discussed. Take a moment at the end of the meeting to confirm that you covered all items. Some general observations about various aspects of the agenda follow for your consideration.

Assumptions. Making assumptions about what the home buyers understand is risky. Expecting, for instance, that home buyers understand why it sometimes appears that "nothing is happening" sets the clients and the builder up for conflict. Take time to explain that such days occur in the construction of every home and give some examples of why. When buyers are prepared for the normal events of construction, they can enjoy their involvement in the building process. Additionally, they will be more likely to believe you later because things you told them happened as you said they would.

Budget. Every home buyer has a budget, even someone building a three million dollar house. Some clients are sensitive about their financial limitations, so be diplomatic about this topic. Avoid any suggestion that their home is low budget, ordinary, or lacking in special touches. Be ready to offer alternatives to accomplish desired results.

Change Requests. Whatever your company policy and schedule for change requests is, discuss it in a forthright manner at the preconstruction conference. Chances are the clients have heard about this from their sales person, read about it in the homeowner manual, and heard about it again during the design and selection stage. Review it again.

Point out that a home is a process. Years after they move in, most home buyers are still thinking of details they would do differently. Homeowners continually discover new likes and dislikes, lifestyles, and tastes change. Few homeowners ever feel their home is "finished," and your clients should not expect that either. Forewarned of this, they are less likely to become angry when you deny a change they think of too late for reasonable implementation.

Quality. If your home buyers notice a detail that disappoints them, they will not rest until they have told someone about it. Such items can be the beginning of serious conflict. By describing for the buyers your quality management steps, how and when inspections of work in progress occur, and the procedures for correcting errors or omissions, you can prevent problems.

Point out that a home is one of the few products that the purchaser can watch being created. While every manufacturing process might include an occasional error, customers do not usually see them occur. Corrections are made before the goods are delivered to stores for distribution. A home is unique in that it is available for viewing every step through its creation. Establish this understanding early so when such things happen, home buyers are not alarmed.

Explain your procedures for corrections, pointing out that the individual whose services are required may be unavailable for days or even weeks. When such questions arise, provide the home buyers with a prompt response and a realistic commitment on when the correction will occur. If the item is within your standards, explain this with equal promptness. This day-to-day management of buyer communications makes the difference between receiving referrals and suffering the effects of a deteriorating relationship.

Site Visits. Many builders express frustration with client interference during construction. With a purchase of this significance and with a process so readily available for viewing, home buyers naturally want to be involved. Questions and concerns are inevitable. Unless you outline procedures for managing these typical events, home buyers will create their methods. Some home buyers will not follow your system even if you describe it for them, but none of them can follow a system that they do not know.

Avoid the unrealistic and futile effort to keep buyers off the site. Instead, emphasize company policies for site visits and the need for safety, appropriate communication, and documentation. Candidly explain that your trade contractor agreements stipulate that alterations to plans or specs are not permitted without your authorization. Point out, for example, that a change in plumbing can impact cabinets, interior trim, and hardware. Uncoordinated and spontaneous changes can cause chaos, delays, and expense. Describe how you want your clients to channel questions, then, make certain that system produces answers for them.

Many small volume builders have discovered that scheduling time to meet with clients at the site once each week or two maintains the home buyers' comfort level and reduces problems. Often, if buyers know they can ask their questions, they resist interfering with work in progress. While this level of attention is probably impractical on high-volume sites, a good system for managing questions still helps tremendously. The key is that the client's question is respected, taken seriously, and responded to promptly.

Something's Missing. At some point during construction nearly every home buyer visits the new home and thinks "Wait a minute, weren't we supposed to have . . . ?" The swirling details and decisions that lead up to the construction of a new home often get mixed up in client memories. Just as often, the company omits a promised item. Prepare your home buyers for such occurrences. Describe what you would like them to do if they believe you have omitted something they ordered.

"The first thing to do is get your paperwork out and confirm that the item is listed. I'm going to build your home according to what is in this file. If an item is included, I should install it. If it is not in these documents, you chose not to order it. So always check here first. If you find I've made a mistake, notify me immediately by contacting your sales person. If you aren't sure, we'd rather check on it for you during construction than discover at delivery that we missed something."

When a system to handle "problems" exists, they do not seem like problems and everyone remains calm.

Conclusion

As the meeting progresses, note details that need further attention. Make your notes detailed and specific; record more than you think you will need to know. What seems clear while your buyers are sitting in front of you fades from memory when hundreds of other details compete for your attention in the days after this meeting. Review this list at the end of the meeting and set times to have answers.

In concluding the preconstruction conference, prepare the clients for the next regularly scheduled meeting—in this case, the frame stage tour. Thank them again for their time, shake hands, and walk them to the door. Clients should leave the preconstruction conference feeling your company was the right choice for them; they should be glad you are in charge of building their new home.

Follow Through

Reliability is an essential component of trust. Meet your commitments to get back to your clients even if all you do is tell them you are still working on the issue. If the home buyers had some items to complete and you have not heard form them by their deadline, contact them to check on progress. As you perform follow-up work, note the answers and when you passed them along to the home buyers. A confirming memo is appropriate in some cases. The builder and the buyers are now working off the same page. The buyers are informed, and their expectations of the construction process are realistic. Most important, a pattern is established for future communications.

10 Predictable Situations

Planned procedures describe the ideal, outlining the pattern that events would take place if everything goes according to your intentions. When you add clients to this process, some variations are to be expected. However, experience identifies some common occurrences and gives home building professionals a chance to prepare for them.

Change Requests

No law prohibits accepting a change order at the preconstruction conference. On the other hand, the point of this meeting is to conduct a comprehensive review of how you will build the home, not to have another design or selection meeting. Somewhere between the two extremes—no changes accepted and any changes accepted—your company needs to find a comfortable position.

The company position on this subject may be based on when the company applies for the building permit in relation to the preconstruction conference, how the system for ordering materials and labor operates, and how difficult it is to make changes at the last minute.

Some companies compromise by prohibiting structural changes but accepting non-structural and cosmetic changes. Sometimes the client wants a change that generates income for the company.

Another option is to inform the home buyers that they should request the preconstruction conference appointment when they are certain that all decisions about their home are complete.

If changes are accepted, other necessary decisions include policies on collecting payment for them and whether administrative fees apply. The key to success with whatever position the company chooses is to explain it to the home buyers before the preconstruction conference is scheduled.

Checkbook Amnesia

One change order at a cost of $892 remains to be signed and paid. At the preconstruction conference, the home buyers pulls out a checkbook only to discover the pad of checks is empty or the checkbook was left "in my other coat."

Either of these can happen to any honest person. They can also be contrived events when a client wants the change but is out of funds at the moment or believes the price is too high. Because intentions are difficult to know with certainty, assume the mistake is an honest one and courteously clarify what the deadline is for payment and that nonpayment will mean the change will be left out of the home.

"Not a problem Mr. Jones. When can you get a check to us? . . . Fine, then what I can do is hold this change order until Friday at 6:00 pm. Otherwise, should you decide for any reason not to add this change, forget about paying for this and the change order will simply expire and not apply to the home." Call the client close to the expiration time to confirm that you are voiding the change order. If payment does not promptly appear, fax a copy of the voided change order.

Delivery Date

Despite repeated explanations (and written descriptions in your homeowner manual), an occasional home buyer will return again and again to their hope that you will complete their new home before the holidays, school starting, the job transfer date, the summer solstice—fill in any particular event.

Because the homeowner manual carefully explains the company position on this topic and the sales person has been well rehearsed in how to talk about this aspect of home construction, you can easily reinforce correct information.

Avoid falling into the trap of committing to "try to get the home done" by the requested date. Giving in to unrealistic delivery date hopes to make clients smile at the meeting will prove costly later when you disappoint them, and they conclude you lied to them.

Insist on facing reality; we have a target range of dates, which will move. We will keep you informed of this moving range of dates and ultimately provide a firm date a minimum of 30 (more if possible) days before delivery.

Error in Paperwork

You are progressing through the agenda, reviewing plans and specifications efficiently, and enjoying the conversations with your clients. Suddenly, the conversation turns from smiles to frowns, and several people are talking at once. Apparently something is wrong in the paperwork. Cynics might ask whether the clients are trying to sneak in a back-door change order. Save your energy and skip worrying about this possibility. Your challenge is getting the paperwork correct and signed so you can build the home.

Stay calm and friendly. Avoid assuming the client is mistaken; errors in paperwork do happen. "We'll get this straightened out." Go to the original change request, selection sheet, working drawings, or meeting notes—whatever shows the beginning of the confusion. Trace each step to look for where information was omitted, transposed, or tangled up. Your goal is not to affix blame but to understand what should be in the documents and how any recurrence might be prevented.

Often, more training is needed for the sales or design center staff in how to describe what the home buyers are ordering. If the descriptions are incomplete, someone in purchasing or drafting might fill in the blanks, leading to a mismatch between the dream of the home buyer and the company's paperwork.

Incomplete Selections

As is the case with change requests, no law exists that prohibits builders from starting construction even though some choices about the home remain incomplete. The issue is one of operational style. What risks does the company take and how much extra work is created? Balance these issues with what your clients have been led to expect and the reasons their choices are incomplete. Options include policies such as these:

- Identify selections that are required before the preconstruction conference and separate them from those that can be finalized later. When the required first phase of selections are made, schedule the preconstruction conference. Follow through with the sales person or design center representative should be part of the normal routine to ensure the remaining choices are communicated in a timely manner to those who need the information.
- If required selections are incomplete, simply postpone the meeting.
- If one or two choices remain, you might schedule the preconstruction conference with the understanding that the home buyers will provide their final decisions at the meeting.

Clarity as to time tables and repercussions is essential. A user-friendly description of the selection process in your homeowner manual can forestall problems in this area. If the majority of your clients can work comfortably within your policies, the policies are probably reasonable. If most home buyers complain and decisions are chronically late, aggravating everyone involved, your company needs to examine the selection system and possibly revise the schedule.

Avoid creating operational chaos by stating a policy and then violating it for aggressive clients while enforcing it for others. Sales and construction personnel should provide consistent information on this issue to all home buyers.

Site-Related Issues

The preconstruction conference has gone well. You've confirmed details of the plans and selections, answered many questions, and described the construction process. Standing on the sloping lot, the home buyers mention, for the second time, that they want a flat backyard. "I want a large vegetable garden and space for the kids play set."

Avoid pretending you did not hear this comment. "Mrs. Jones, have you given any thought to how you'll put your garden in on this slope without interfering with the drainage swales we will be installing?" Asking this question does two things for you. First, it shows the homeowner you intend to install drainage swales, not prepare the site for a garden. Second, the conversation that follows offers you the chance to make suggestions to address both goals and give the client some ideas they can use later.

You main goal is to prevent any wishful thinking on the part of the home buyers that you will create a flat lot where a sloped one exists. Candor works best for such issues. Whether the question has to do with the orientation of the home, configuration of the drive, location of utility junction, or mail boxes, get the facts out clearly, courteously, and early.

Surprise Issues

Particularly if a client has an aggressive personality, by the end of a meeting that has perhaps lasted several hours, your thinking may have been influenced. When the question is unique and you have no idea what position your company would want you to take, take time to think.

Make note of the question, saying "That's an important issue. I'll research it and get back with you Friday afternoon with an answer." Some time away from the meeting environment to research and reflect will produce a better response to unusual issues.

When a contract to build a new home is signed, part of the product being sold is the experience of watching the new home being built. The process has powerful appeal—one a resale home cannot duplicate, and one builders can turn into an advantage by managing it effectively. A well-managed preconstruction conference is an important step to achieving that goal.

4

Frame Stage Tour

Quality Inside the Walls

Frame stage tours involve only the home buyers and the superintendent, take place in a home under construction where noise and dust are likely but sitting down is not, and usually last from 20 to 40 minutes. Because of these informal circumstances, the frame stage tour's contribution to client satisfaction can be overlooked. Consider what this meeting means to the home buyers.

The frame stage tour is the home buyers' opportunity to have your undivided attention, to ask questions about their home, and have you point out the quality features your company builds into the walls of their home. Just as the preconstruction conference expanded trust from the sales person to you, this meeting extends that trust to the home itself.

By planning a frame stage tour as part of your customer relations efforts, you address the client's concerns in a predictable and orderly manner. For many home buyers, knowing they have a scheduled meeting in which they can discuss their concerns prevents them from contacting the company repeatedly with one or two questions. Think of the frame stage tour as an investment in a healthy relationship with your home buyers; give it the attention it deserves.

Policies and Procedures

The frame stage tour usually occurs when rough mechanicals are complete, or nearly so, and prior to the insulation and drywall stages. Therefore, the window of time for conducting this meeting is short and the notice to the clients may likewise be short. Alert home buyers to this fact early. The sales person can mention it in an overview of the process, and the conclusion of the preconstruction conference is another good time to mention it.

Schedule

Despite the short time frame, scheduling this meeting can be easier because the appointment involves fewer people. In many cases, just one of the home buyers attends, although both should be invited. Appointments are frequently set for before or after the client's work day or may occur over the lunch hour. (Work colleagues sometimes tag along—offering an astute superintendent the chance to make a good impression on another potential buyer.)

The builder's sales person is usually welcome to attend, but few companies require that the sales person be involved. When possible, if the sales person can stop by for a moment to show interest, the effect is positive. Home buyers, understandably, enjoy all this attention.

In a few instances, the superintendent and sales person may conclude that the sales person should attend—either to foster the clients' comfort or to head off potential problems with an aggressive client, or one prone to misquoting what the sales person promised.

When you contact the clients to schedule this appointment, have some preferred days and times in mind. Offer a choice of two possible times and proceed from there. Allow 20–45 minutes for the frame stage tour, depending on the size of the home and your client's personality. If the preconstruction conference ran long because the home buyer had a lot of questions or is detail oriented, block out extra time for this meeting.

Remind the clients that the homesite will be dusty (muddy, snowy, or whatever) so they can dress appropriately or bring extra footwear. Recommend that children not attend this meeting for safety reasons. Mention that this is an excellent opportunity to ask questions and a written list is a good idea. Ask that they bring their homeowner manual as well.

Prepare

Although to you this meeting may seem like just one more item on a long list of things to do, it is significant to the clients. Failing to prepare properly, arriving late, or rushing through the home, not taking the time to point out quality steps in the construction and confirm selections and change orders, means you miss a valuable opportunity.

Prepare for the frame stage tour with steps similar to the preconstruction conference. Review the file and check in with the sales person for updates about the home buyers. One additional preparation step—getting the home site ready—is critical. Confirm the following steps:

- Delivered materials should be stored neatly and securely. These components will eventually make up the home; the client will want to see them being respected and protected from damage.
- Scraps and trash should be removed and the home itself swept. If everyone who works on the home site cleans up scraps and debris before leaving, the construction area will stay neater and safer at all times.
- Safety considerations should be checked and addressed, appropriate rails installed and other protective measures taken.
- Compare the home to the information in the file. Is anything missing or incorrect?
- What is the status of any issue the home buyers have raised?
- Do you have any questions for the home buyers? If so, note them on the agenda.
- How does the surrounding area look? Muddy streets, tilting portable toilets, and weathered stacks of unused materials should be corrected as soon as possible.
- Similarly, loud radios, squealing tires, and screamed obscenities set an "anything goes" tone on the job. Home buyers are reassured that someone who respects the work is in control. Everything counts.

Prepare the necessary paperwork. A sample frame stage tour agenda is shown in Figure 11.1 to help develop your list of topics. This file is helpful in resolving any questions. Again, remember to bring your homeowner manual and arrive early for the appointment so you have a few minutes to focus on the home, gather your thoughts, and greet the home buyers when they arrive.

Conduct

A common tendency is to show up for the frame stage tour and stroll around the home more or less haphazardly.

Formalize the frame stage tour by following a route that closely matches that of the orientation yet to come. Greet your clients at the street when they arrive, tour the exterior of the home first, enter through the front door, and end in their future kitchen. The reasons for this itinerary are described in detail in the Part on orientations.

FIGURE 11.1 Sample Frame Stage Tour Agenda

Date _____

Purchasers _____

Address _____

Lot _____ Plan _____

A construction tour was completed on this date to review topics listed below and confirm correct installation of selections visible in the home at this time. Some items listed on selection sheets or described in change orders may not be apparent at this stage of construction.

Exterior
- ☐ Elevation
- ☐ Exterior finish materials
- ☐ Meter locations
- ☐ Air conditioner condenser location
- ☐ Patio/deck
- ☐ Hose bib locations
- ☐ Property boundaries
- ☐ Drainage swales
- ☐ Driveway
- ☐ Sidewalk
- ☐ Fence installation

Interior
- ☐ Foundation system
- ☐ Beams and supports
- ☐ Framing options
- ☐ Floor system
- ☐ Doors and windows
- ☐ Ceiling details
- ☐ Engineered components
- ☐ Trusses
- ☐ Roof sheathing
- ☐ Flashing
- ☐ House wrap
- ☐ Electrical options
- ☐ HVAC options

- ☐ Plumbing options
- ☐ Appliances
- ☐ Built-ins
- ☐ Basement floor
- ☐ Underground services

Questions for follow up:

_____

_____

_____

_____

_____

_____

_____

_____

_____

_____

Purchaser _____

Date _____

Purchaser _____

Date _____

Builder _____

Date _____

Introduction

As you did in the preconstruction conference, begin with an introduction that thanks the clients for taking time to meet with you and reviews the purpose of the meeting.

"I want to thank you for once again taking time to meet with me. These meetings have proven their value to me many times. As your homeowner manual describes, we invited you out today to confirm details in the home so far, answer any questions you have, and give me a chance to show you the quality of construction inside your walls."

Ask that the home buyers stay together and stay with you. Reinforce key points about safety before you get started. In particular, repeat the suggestions that they look in the direction they are walking and avoid stepping backwards at any time.

Agenda

Reviewing the file and walking through the home to confirm selections are installed correctly should make the client's selections fresh in your mind. As you enter each area or room, call attention to any optional or custom features the home buyers ordered. In particular, confirm that the number and location of optional phone, cable, and electrical outlets is correct.

Follow this confirmation with general information about the construction techniques visible in the room. After you have conducted a few of these, you will find that each floor plan has certain rooms that work best for calling attention to certain items. For instance, discuss roof trusses from a vantage point where they are easily seen. As you will see with the orientation, the physical items in the home support your memory.

Pause once or twice to check your printed agenda and confirm you have covered what you intended. Give your clients time to ask questions and make comments. If an issue comes up you cannot resolve on the spot, list it on the agenda for further investigation and note when you will update the clients on your progress.

Avoid talking about competitors in any negative way. While it is acceptable to say "One unique thing we do here at [Builder] that you seldom see in our region is. . . ." but avoid comments such as "You should be glad you didn't buy from [Builder down the street]; their quality really stinks."

Conclusion

Wrap up the frame stage tour by reviewing any items you noted for investigation, reiterating the date you will get back to the clients. Remind them of the next regular meeting—the orientation.

This is a good time to touch on some key points about the orientation, such as that it takes approximately 2 hours, is a chance to learn about use and care of the home and confirm completion and good condition. Alert the clients to expect considerable activity by many people during the last few days just before the orientation, and explain that this is normal.

Ask whether they have any questions. Thank them again for their time and walk them back to their car.

Follow Through

Whenever you meet with a homeowner, have a pen and notepad handy. This valuable habit serves three purposes:

1. A written note helps you remember your follow-up tasks.
2. When clients see you making detailed records, they feel confident those details will be properly addressed.
3. If you ever need to defend yourself or your company, documentation will be essential.

Client meetings, supported with printed agendas offer an automatic and standardized place to record notes. Using these notes effectively increases their value. Immediately after your client meeting, review the notes, prioritize any outstanding issues, and decide what steps you need to take to resolve each.

12 Predictable Situations

Approach the frame stage tour with the expectation that a few follow-up items will result. Think of the resulting work as saving you even more time later. Often you will be surprised to leave this meeting knowing all is well, and your clients are delighted with their new home. Being prepared for topics that commonly arise can also help you be more successful with your frame stage tours.

Buyers Expect an Item Not Ordered

Remember at the preconstruction conference when you discussed the steps the home buyers should take if they believe something they ordered is missing? Here's where that preparation pays off.

Whether they recall that part of the preconstruction conference or not, you can repeat the information, and even demonstrate. Avoid assuming the clients are mistaken and take a let's-figure-this-out-together approach. "What we need to do first is look at the paperwork in the file and see what is on order for your home."

If after checking the paperwork it turns out you have made the error, be a good sport about it—avoid any appearance of annoyance. Take a "Glad we caught that now" attitude. After all, finding such oversights is one of the purposes of the frame stage tour.

If the home buyers were mistaken, be equally gracious. Consider whether a late change order can be used to add the item. This possibility must work within normal company policies. Use common sense, however, and make appropriate exceptions when circumstances justify bending the rules.

Buyers' Lists

Clients often fax, email, or drop off a list of instructions that range from "get the dead bug out of the rough opening for the garage window" to "install roof shingles." After receiving such a list, many are tempted to respond, "We probably would have thought of that!"

Tossing home buyer lists into a desk draw and ignoring them is disrespectful and can be embarrassing and expensive. Hidden among such suggestions as "connect electrical service," you may find things of which you were unaware such as "the fireplace is in the wrong room" or "we ordered a blue bathtub and an almond one was delivered." Hearing an "I told you so" from a frustrated client is an unpleasant experience and should be avoided whenever possible.

When the sales person forwards a list from a home buyer just before the frame stage tour, review it in preparation for the meeting so you can respond to each item. Note your answer and attach a copy to the frame stage tour agenda for your permanent records on the home.

Buyers Live Out of State

Home buyers who live far away are most likely to miss their frame stage tour than any of the other client meetings. Before you get excited at having regained the time the frame stage tour would have taken, think about this from the client's perspective. Find a way to conduct some version of this tour.

Photos, videotape, faxed updates, or even just a conference call all go a long way toward making your clients feel involved and important. Another possibility is conducting at least the informational portion of the frame stage tour on someone else's home when the buyers are in town. Although this is not their home, in general, your construction practices should be the same.

The emotional experience during the home building process is as important to future referrals as the physical product quality. Remember that if only one of the buyers attends, ask about the partner and send greetings to him or her.

Change Requests

Company policy or the cut-off schedule on change orders will determine how you respond when home buyers ask to make further changes to their home during the frame stage tour. Ideally, clients are well informed about these policies and resist asking for things you cannot do. At the same time, show some discretion in this area.

If you have an "off with their heads" attitude, perhaps building a new home yourself will get you in touch with reality, if not empathy. Rarely does anyone go through the home building process without wishing they had ordered something different somewhere in the home. Use common sense and be flexible when you can do so without creating chaos in the field.

For instance, if your electrician is still working in the home, or even just down the street, and your client requests two more outlets in the basement, arbitrarily saying no may cost you more time and effort in the long run than arranging for this change. However, if your clients decide to extend the back of the foundation out another 3 feet, it makes sense to deny that request. If any changes at all are approved, document them and obtain the required signatures and payment before proceeding with the change.

Error in the Home

If your home buyers say "We ordered the family room fireplace, not the living room fireplace," two possibilities exist. First, the home buyers are correct; second, they are not. Either way, your response must be respectful. "Let's look at the file and see where we got off track here."

The use of "we" is important. Your goal is to keep this conversation friendly and avoid implying that the home buyers are causing you extra work. Even if you are absolutely positive the home is correct as it stands, avoid overbearing responses such as "No you didn't, that's not what's in my paperwork." If it turns out the home buyers are mistaken, your next concern is to mitigate any embarrassment they may feel.

If the fireplace being in the living room completely destroys any possibility they will ever have a moment's enjoyment in this home, you might be able to offer a price for changing it. This more drastic step depends on your company's operational style and how flexible your construction schedule is. On the other hand, sometimes after they think things over for a day or so, they remember why they made the decision they did and become comfortable with it as it is.

Quality Debate

"There's a knot hole in this stud; I want it replaced" is a classic example of quality issues likely to come up during the frame stage tour. Realistically, chances that you will invite home buyers to tour their new home during construction without having an occasional discussion about quality is unlikely. (Imagine your invitation—"Come out and see your home, but don't form any opinions about it.")

Rather than snapping back a quick "no" supplemented with a severe frown, consider this approach. "Well, let's take a look at what we're asking this stud to do. Actually, it is only going to hold up the drywall at the back of the closet. These other three in the corner do the real work, they help support the weight of the doors. This knot hole is nothing to be concerned about. In fact, we can find them in the framing of every home out here."

Trades

Trade personnel will frequently be working in or near the home where you are conducting the frame stage tour. Materials may be delivered (such as your roofer stocking a roof across the street), or excavation or grading may be in progress on adjacent lots. The noise of such activities can make conversations difficult during the frame stage tour.

Ideally, anyone working right in the home you are touring can take a short break or at least do some quiet work. Minimally, anyone on the job should turn off radios and shut down power tools. At all times, trade personnel should show respect for the homes in which they work. A well-run job site is one where all workers observe appropriate courtesies—of the property, each other, and the clients.

Speaking of trades, a common concern superintendents have are private arrangements home buyers try to make with trade contractors. Buyers may try to make unauthorized field changes or side deals with the folks working in their home. Prevention involves working from both sides: home buyers and trades. You outlined for the home buyer how to ask questions or request changes at the preconstruction conference. Review these procedures again at the frame stage tour.

Behind the scenes, reinforce your efforts by educating your trade contractors. Your contracts with them should clearly state your policy on changes, additions, or deletions. If approached by a home buyer requesting some change, the trade contractor can courteously explain that all changes must be authorized in writing by the company. Teach trades people to say "Talk to sales" in a friendly voice.

Home Buyer Orientation
Golden Opportunity

Well-done, home buyer orientations look easy. When a competent orientation representative presents a new home to clients, the meeting flows smoothly. Such a meeting includes a bit of theater, a wealth of useful information, and a fair examination of the home. Orientations work best when their focus is on education and celebration. In the end, the home buyers conclude that they got a valuable return on the time invested in the orientation appointment. The benefits do not stop here. Your company stands to gain tremendous advantages from sound management of the home delivery process.

Walking-Talking Billboard

Few of us go through moving without telling everyone who will listen. The work, the crises, the inconveniences, the cost, the outrage, and the funny events generate many conversations. For days before, during, and after their move, home buyers talk of little else. The preparations absorb their time and conversations with family, friends, co-workers, and strangers. During these conversations, your company's name is likely to come up. These clients are walking-talking billboards for your company. By polishing your delivery process, you reap benefits only satisfied homeowners can create. Few ad campaigns convince prospective buyers as quickly as a homeowner who says "[Builder] treated us well. We're glad we bought our home from them."

Warranty Relationship

Besides the benefits of positive word-of-mouth, a smooth orientation process produces a healthy relationship between homeowners and the warranty department. When homeowners know how to use and care for their home, they make fewer phone calls to the warranty office with questions. When homeowners understand the procedures for reporting warranty items, they are more likely to follow those procedures. And when homeowners conclude they were treated fairly by their builder, they request reasonable warranty services rather than submitting revenge lists. The result of all these conditions is greater efficiency in the warranty office: better service for all homeowners at a lower cost to the builder and trades.

Transition from Buying to Owning

Experts observe that human beings can form a habit after repeating a behavior for as little as 21 days. By the time they close on their new home, most clients have behaved as home buyers for months. As home buyers, when they want something involving the home, they contact the builder. The builder responds. This pattern is repeated many times. By the time of the closing, behaving like a home buyer is a well-established habit.

The closing is the official signal that this buyer behavior should now change to owner behavior. Responsibility for the home should shift from the builder to the homeowners. Yet, after months of behaving in buyer mode, many clients have difficulty changing that habit. By creating a bit of ritual—a ceremony—that marks the change from buyer to owner, you can help your home buyers make this transition.

The orientation process addresses all of these objectives. To handle this assignment well requires considerable study, much thought, and continuous polishing. Acquiring the knowledge required to do orientations effectively is a challenge. Insights about home buyers, detailed knowledge about the community, your company's product, and well thought-out responses for predictable situations are essential to this assignment.

13

Policies and Procedures

H ome buyer emotions combined with the vast number of details to address make the orientation one of the most challenging of client meetings. However, orientations are also one of most rewarding. Sharing the excitement of home buyers who are pleased with their new home is immensely gratifying. When all the systems are working as they should, the orientation meeting is quite enjoyable.

Schedule

In addition to the standard scheduling issues outlined in Chapter 6, orientations should be done in day light. For most companies, offering appointments Monday through Friday, 8:00 a.m. to 3:00 p.m. works acceptably. In some climates, winter hours vary from other seasons due to fading natural light. Some builders designate certain days of the week for orientation appointments in specified subdivisions. A few companies offer morning appointments on Saturdays. This is fine as long as you are comfortable answering the question "Why can you do orientations on Saturday but not warranty repair appointments?"

Another aspect of orientation scheduling to consider is how far in advance of the closing should the orientation occur? Avoid having the orientation at 9:00 a.m., the closing at 11:00 a.m., and the move-in at 1:00 p.m. Field personnel deserve time to react to the orientation list, and in most cases, 3 to 5 days is adequate to complete the list and deliver a finished home.

While these policies must accommodate a variety of buyer circumstances, having a standard framework results in more orderly processes. Provide your buyers with scheduling information early; these points can be covered in your homeowner manual.

When setting the appointment with the home buyers, review key points to prepare them for this meeting. These might include any or all of the following:

- These meetings show the home and confirm correct completion.
- The orientation will take approximately 2 hours.

- The agenda includes several hundred details; please attend alone to focus attention on the information presented.
- The individual who will conduct the meeting is <name> and any last minute items will be addressed by <name>.
- Response time on these items is usually 10 work days or less.
- Follow-up procedure includes a phone call or personal visit.
- You can find more information and copies of forms in the homeowner manual.
- Review "Caring for your home" in the homeowner manual and bring questions.
- You will be touring the exterior; wear comfortable clothing for the weather and shoes that can get dirty. We provide paper "booties" to cover them when we go inside.
- A last minute flurry of activity is normal; many people will work in the home during the last several days leading up to this meeting. They are fine tuning and making final adjustments or installations.

Prepare

As with the other client meetings, preparing ahead of time is critical. Keep these suggestions in mind.

- Confirm that you know the location of the home and how to get to it on time.
- Be familiar with the floor plan—visiting the showhome or the actual home, if no showhome exists.
- Review selection sheets and change orders for the home.
- If some unique products are included, check manufacturer information and be ready to speak about them accurately and with confidence.
- Check with sales and construction to learn about any last minute issues.
- If you are aware of a question or concern, try to get an answer or at least an update prior to the orientation.

Conduct

Traditional training would include following someone else through a few orientations and having that individual follow you a few times as well. This casual approach worked fine 20 years ago. Today's sophisticated buyers expect something more extensive and polished. Although observing orientations by others is valuable, don't assume that the individuals you observe are covering all relevant information or using the best techniques.

The content of your presentation should evolve based on a combination of observation of orientations by others and systematic research. Develop a style based on your personality, solid information, and respect for your buyers. Your goals in observing others are to gain a sense of the overall presentation, listen for useful bits of information, and watch for effective techniques. Notice the home buyers' reactions to the information presented and the questions they ask.

Then, conduct your own research to continue improving the content and style of your presentation. After some practice, ask some of the veterans you observed to review and provide feedback. Even after dozens of orientations, you should continue to improve. New information is always available, and polishing communication techniques is never-ending.

Itinerary

Several years ago I observed an orientation involving a busy superintendent and an elderly couple. The superintendent was rattling off a list of things the builder would not repair before the home buyers were completely out of their car. As I watched and listened, I could not help thinking "This should be more fun—there's got to be a better way." In my view, the itinerary described here is that better way.

The itinerary is the route around and through the home. Without a strategic itinerary, the route taken through the home can be haphazard and is likely to vary from home to home. Such orientations often seem as if they are conducted by a butterfly, flitting about the home at random. The advantages of replacing this accidental approach with a consistent itinerary are worth mentioning:

- When each orientation follows the same itinerary, you reduce the chance that you will overlook something.
- A standard pattern and time table evolves; you know how long each segment should take and can gauge whether the discussion is off track.
- Technicians who work in the home after the orientation can find items easily when they are listed in a standard order.
- Basing the orientation on a well-considered itinerary allows you to present the home in the best possible order and celebrate the event with the buyers.

Begin at the Street. An itinerary that produces excellent results begins with greeting the buyers at the street. This approach makes use of several insights about home buyers and the nature of the orientation process (and is another good reason for you to arrive early).

If you greet the buyers at the street, as they get out of their vehicle, you can welcome them, exchange the normal amenities, and then pause to look at the house. Let the buyers savor this moment.

Turning their attention to the new home, you might say "Congratulations, Mr. and Mrs. Jones. Here's your new home. Your exterior colors look wonderful on this elevation. You've done a great job in your selections." Or perhaps you are more comfortable describing the home a bit. "Your new home is our Wellington plan. You selected the B elevation and added a bay window to the living room. This makes a beautiful combination and I especially like the stone accent you added." (Note that the garage overhead doors should be closed at this point. As useful as garages are, they are not all that attractive.)

Avoid being in such a hurry that this gratifying moment is lost. Simply looking at the home for these few seconds accomplishes several important things for your home buyers. First, the whole-house moment provides a healthy perspective for the rest of your home tour. Viewing the home from the street fixes the size of it in the home buyers' minds. If you subsequently note a few minor items for attention, they are seen in perspective— against the image of the entire home.

Next, notice the difference between this approach and the itinerary that takes buyers directly to the kitchen, where traditionally the orientation began with a review of the manufacturers' materials about appliances. Buyers often look around or even wander off, paying little attention to information about the appliance warranties. The garbage disposal warranty is a tedious beginning to what should be an exciting time for the buyers. Many buyers struggle to break free to look at the whole house. The moment at the street helps satisfy this desire.

This ceremonial moment also begins the vital transition from buying to owning. Compare the visual and emotional impact of this moment to sitting in an unfamiliar room, separated from the home, signing 75 or so documents as a stranger (the closing agent) shuffles papers and checks around. Which experience is more likely to produce a sense of owning that new home?

Exterior First. The moment at the street leads naturally into starting your presentation there. As you discuss the home's exterior, follow a set pattern, such as going clockwise. In turn, discuss each exterior agenda item. The Sample Agenda in Figure 13.1 offers suggestions. Remember that the emphasis is education: help your clients understand how each component of their home works, what to expect from it long term, how to care for it, and what the builder's limited warranty commitments are.

Front Entrance. After completing a tour of the exterior, return to the front of the home. Enter the home through the front door—as if the home buyers are guests. Exteriors are not as finely detailed or tightly finished as interiors. After looking at the outside for 15 to 20 minutes, the sparkling interior looks even better. Shoes are usually removed or covered with "booties" as everyone enters the home.

Show and discuss the entry features (see the Sample Agenda in Figure 13.1 for potential topics). Next, go to the master bedroom, proceeding through the other bedrooms, bathrooms, garage, basement, living room, dining room, family room, and so on. Specifics will vary according to the geography of the floor plan.

Some orientation veterans prefer to go from the entry area directly to the basement, then proceed to the bedrooms. If this seems logical to you, do so. The critical points are exterior first, enter through the front door, kitchen last.

Kitchen Last. Show the kitchen last. You will arrive with the buyers' confidence high and anxiety low. This brings us to one more reason to update the traditional kitchen-first itinerary. Another negative associated with starting in the kitchen is the paranoia-inducing inspection for cosmetic damage.

Note legitimate items, whether cosmetic or functional. In fact, you should volunteer to note any item that does not meet your company's promised standards, including cosmetic items. After all, your company's name is on this home. Watch with special care for those items that might cause conflict later, such as cosmetic damages. However, starting with uninteresting paperwork and progressing to nervous inspection of cosmetic surfaces turns what should be a celebration into boring work at best, and a nerve wracking challenge at worst.

As if that's not bad enough, the buyers' habit (which the traditional itinerary helps to create) of looking at every kitchen surface from a distance of three inches continues through the rest of the home. This leads to either denials of requested items or a long list of minute items that will have technicians rolling their eyes. You also risk creating a negative impression of poor quality—just look at that long list! Such close inspection often continues through the warranty period, creating frustration for homeowners and warranty staff alike. The orientation teaches the buyers how to evaluate their home and needs to be done with a reasonable perspective, within an educational context.

End the tour of the home in the kitchen with an orderly demonstration of kitchen features. Show how appliances work and discuss care of surfaces. Use the counter space to review paperwork, briefly reviewing the manufacturer's literature you organized before the buyers arrived.

Agenda

To develop your orientation agenda, begin with the Sample Agenda shown in Figure 13.1. Adjust the list of topics to reflect your company's products and circumstances. Where appropriate, list the subpoints you want to remember to discuss under each topic. Review the Component sheets (Figure 5.2) you completed to identify key points. If necessary, write out details of which you are unsure and practice your descriptions until you feel confident. Once your core presentation is under control, develop your introduction and conclusion. You will find it easier to create these two important elements of your presentation when you know what that presentation includes. Details follow the sample agenda.

Go to an empty home—alone—and rehearse, out loud. You will be surprised at how much information you have to cover, and equally surprised to discover how little time each item actually takes if the key points are well organized. Remember that the physical items in the home will be in front of you; the home itself helps you remember what to talk about. Your goal is to become comfortable covering three aspects for each topic: use and care, long-term performance, and warranty coverage.

For more complex systems, such as the furnace, water heater, and fireplace, organize your descriptions in a logical order: top to bottom, right to left, or so on. Keep operating steps in sequence. Your buyers may be unfamiliar with the item; jumping around is confusing, takes longer, and runs the risk that you will omit something.

As you rehearse, note a few topics of which you need more study. When you find yourself struggling with how to explain something, the cause will usually be that you have not yet mastered the information and need to study your material. If that does not solve the problem, contact an expert and talk about it. Your electrician, for example, will be happy to teach you how to explain the breaker panel.

When complete, your written agenda guides your rehearsals and will be useful when you get promoted and need to train your replacement.

Introduction

Because the introduction and conclusion are vital to successful orientations, pay special attention these parts of the meeting. While you should be flexible to specific client needs and personalities, having a firm framework for the orientation improves the likelihood of your success.

A strong introduction impresses the buyers and puts you in charge. Show early on that you have a plan for conducting the orientation. If your home buyers have attended a pre-construction conference and a frame stage tour, they will be expecting this. Minimally, you should cover these points:

- Greet the buyers (including handshakes and business cards as applicable).
- Take a moment to view their new home from the street.

FIGURE 13.1 Sample Orientation Agenda

Exterior
- [ ] Elevation
- [ ] House numbers
- [ ] Property boundaries
- [ ] Water meter and street shut-off
- [ ] Electric meter and main shut-off
- [ ] Gas meter and main shut-off
- [ ] Telephone connection
- [ ] Cable TV connection
- [ ] Final grade complete
- [ ] Drainage, slope, swales
- [ ] Backfill settlement
- [ ] Downspout extensions or splashblocks
- [ ] Installation of landscaping and placement of soil from holes dug for fence, shrubs
- [ ] Erosion excluded from limited warranty
- [ ] Outside faucet protection, remove hoses
- [ ] Sprinkler
      Setting the timer
      Shut down procedures
- [ ] Deck care
- [ ] Cleaning gutters
- [ ] Window weep holes: Importance of cleaning
- [ ] CAUTION: direct vent fireplace exhaust cover gets very hot
- [ ] Outside lights
- [ ] Paint or stain maintenance
- [ ] Caulking a maintenance item
- [ ] Shingles
- [ ] Siding or stucco
- [ ] Masonry
- [ ] Chimney
- [ ] Trim and shutters
- [ ] Exterior doors
- [ ] Protection of exterior concrete slabs
      Seal cracks to prevent water penetration
      Remove ice and snow
      Protect drive and walks from road salt
- [ ] Exterior GFCI outlet
- [ ] Homeowner association design review for changes or additions

Entry
- [ ] Doorbell
- [ ] Walls, ceiling, floor, trim (WCFT)
- [ ] Operate and confirm entry light
- [ ] Check operation of locks and threshold
- [ ] Confirm front door condition

Bedrooms
- [ ] WCFT
- [ ] Doors and doorstops
- [ ] Switched outlet
- [ ] Window and screen: Condition and operation
      Lock operation
      Screen removal
      Manufacturer warranty on seal
      Wax or silicone to lubricate
- [ ] Adjustable registers
- [ ] Keep cold air returns clear
- [ ] Closet
      Doors
      Shelves
      Rod

Bathrooms
- [ ] WCFT
- [ ] Door, doorstop, and privacy lock
- [ ] Window and screen
- [ ] Sink and faucet
- [ ] Run water to check stopper
- [ ] Shut offs
- [ ] Flush toilet
      Water saving features
- [ ] Tub/spa—point jets down, access
- [ ] Shower—shower diverter, shower enclosure, recommend squeegee

FIGURE 13.1 Sample Orientation Agenda (*contd.*)

- ☐ Ground fault circuit interrupter (GFCI)
- ☐ Countertop
- ☐ Cabinets
- ☐ Mirrors
- ☐ Light
- ☐ Run fan
- ☐ Caulk and grout maintenance
- ☐ Avoid abrasive cleaners

Attic Access
- ☐ Caution about walking in attic: disturbing insulation, stepping through ceiling
- ☐ Not for storage
- ☐ Can see daylight through required vents

Stairs
- ☐ Call attention to stringer, probable effects of shrinkage

Thermostat
- ☐ Settings and operation
- ☐ Calibration within 5 degrees

Living Room
- ☐ WCFT
- ☐ Window and screen
- ☐ Switched outlet
- ☐ Effects of humidity and shrinkage

Dining Room
- ☐ WCFT
- ☐ Window and screen
- ☐ Confirm chandelier

Family Room
- ☐ WCFT
- ☐ Window and screen
- ☐ Fireplace
  For atmosphere, inefficient as a heat source
  Demonstrate damper and combustion air
  Discuss glass door use
  Demonstrate gas pilot procedures, if applicable
  New appliance odor

Garage
- ☐ Breaker Panel
- ☐ Demonstrate procedure to reset tripped breaker
- ☐ GFCI circuit NOT FOR FREEZER or garage door opener
- ☐ Check operation of overhead door
- ☐ Locate garage door keys
- ☐ To install opener, reverse latch
- ☐ Installation by others voids warranty
- ☐ Slope of garage floor
- ☐ Avoid hosing garage floor; sweep to clean
- ☐ Seal cracks in slab
- ☐ Door to house and closer
- ☐ Window
- ☐ Furnace and air conditioner
  Combustion air—DO NOT COVER
  Gas shut off
  Demonstrate how to light pilot
  Explain thermal coupler
  How and when to change filter
  Fan safety switch, reattach door securely
  On-off switch
  Fuse—have extra on hand
  A/C condensate line
  Odor—when new or after not being used
- ☐ Water heater
  Combustion air
  Gas shut off
  Pilot and thermal coupler
  Water shut off
  Pop-off valve
  Flu HOT
  Drain at bottom to remove sediment
  Temperature control

Laundry Room
- ☐ WCFT
- ☐ Window and screen
- ☐ Light fixture
- ☐ Shelves or cabinets
- ☐ Connections—drain cover, dryer vent

FIGURE 13.1 Sample Orientation Agenda (*contd.*)

☐ Run a couple of cycles empty to clear lines; repeat at all water sources

☐ Floor covering caution; will receive number for patchwork if needed

Kitchen/Nook

☐ WCFT

☐ Window, screen or patio door

☐ Range/cooktop/oven
Check all burners
New appliance odor
Cost of self-cleaning, steps in operating
Energy savings
Caution about using chemical oven cleaners
Avoid self-cleaning chrome parts
Confirm broiler pan is included
Oven door removal
Cooktop grease catcher

☐ Hood
Filter—clean or replace
Size of bulb

☐ Sink
Run water, check hot water temperature
Shut offs
Demonstrate sprayer
Demonstrate how to clean aerator

☐ Keep countertop dry

☐ Disposal
Run briefly

Reset button or wrench
Run cold water while operating
Clean blades by grinding ice cubes
Freshen with baking soda or citrus rinds
Avoid stringy items: celery, corn silk

☐ Dishwasher
Confirm racks and basket
Discuss settings, energy saving features
Rinse aid dispenser
Confirm that water is on, operate dishwasher
New appliance odor
Hardwood floor damage results from drips

☐ Cabinets
Care and cleaning
Demonstrate adjustable shelves
Confirm doors, drawers, shelves, and hardware

☐ Countertop
Caution about cutting, hot pans, and so on
Effect of shrinkage
Effect of excess water on seams

☐ Floor covering
Caution about moving appliances
Glides on furniture legs
Cleaning method; products to avoid
Caution about excess water

☐ GFCI—locate, remind about freezer in GFCI receptacle

- Review the purposes of the orientation.
- Describe procedures (framing this with something along the lines of "we use a 3-step procedure. . ." is helpful).
- Ensure the buyers that they will receive a copy of the completed paperwork.
- Reinforce the value of your homeowner manual (which is under your arm at this point).

You might want to write your introductory script. You are welcome to begin with the sample in Figure 13.2 and modify it to suit your circumstances. Rehearse until it feels natural. Some situations will require thinking on your feet and on-the-spot adjustments in your standard opening, but your planned introduction will work most of the time.

FIGURE 13.2 Sample Orientation Introduction

Mr. & Mrs. Jones, [shaking hands] welcome to your new home. I'm <name> and I'll be conducting your orientation today. [Provide all parties with your business cards if you are meeting for the first time.] Congratulations. Your new home's complete. [Turn and look at the home. Comment on some aspect of the home to give buyers time to enjoy this moment.]

We want to accomplish two things today. This meeting is intended to educate you about the use and care of your home and its systems. We also want to confirm that the home meets the quality standards displayed in our showhomes [or described in your purchase agreement]. To do this I ask that both of you stay with me as we go through your home room by room following a three-step procedure.

First, in each area, I'll demonstrate features to show you how things work.

Second, we'll discuss your maintenance responsibilities and our warranty commitment. This information is included in your homeowner manual and manufacturer materials you'll receive. We know you have a lot on your mind, and we don't expect you to memorize every detail; you can always look up information later. That's one of the reasons we created our homeowner manual.

Third, we'll look at each area together. I'll make note of any items I see that do not meet [Builder] standards, then ask for your comments or questions. We'll be confirming that cosmetic surfaces are in acceptable condition. I'll remind you of this again at the end of the orientation. We want to take care of any cosmetic repairs that are identified today. Once you move in, attention to cosmetic surfaces will be your responsibility.

We've found this system works efficiently and helps all of us stay organized. At the end of our meeting, you'll have a chance to review the list and you get a copy for your records. Does that sound like a workable plan? . . . Good, then let's get started. [Begin exterior agenda.]

Conclusion

In closing remarks, emphasize the information covered and that you have confirmed the good condition of the home's cosmetic surfaces. Avoid saying "we realize we may have missed something" or "we recognize we may have overlooked some items today" because the homeowners may later interrupt that to include cosmetic damages.

In most cases, three adults just walked through a clean, empty home in daylight with the purpose—among others—of confirming the good condition of cosmetic surfaces. While overlooking a scratch, dent, or some other cosmetic damage is possible, such an oversight is rare.

Builders do make repairs to cosmetic items noted after this meeting (for instance, a stress crack in a window), but to be fair, the choice should be based on a reasonable review of circumstances by the builder. You want to avoid later conflicts about such items. Consider the sample conclusion in Figure 13.3 and then create one for your presentations. Points to cover include the following:

- Display manufacturer warranties.
- Ask the home buyers to review the items you noted on the orientation list.
- Explain the time frame for completion of these items and who is responsible for overseeing that work.
- Sign the orientation forms and provide the home buyers with their copies.

FIGURE 13.3 Sample Orientation Conclusion

Please take a minute to review the list. We noted seven items. The superintendent will resolve each of these, many of them before you move in. If anything remains to be completed after your move-in, we'll contact you to set an appointment. I know you read in our homeowner manual that service appointments are available Monday through Friday, from 7:00 a.m. to 4:00 p.m. Depending on your availability, remaining items are usually completed within 10 work days.

We've looked at how things work in your home, we've discussed many key points about maintenance and warranty coverage. We've also confirmed that [Builder] correctly installed the items and colors you ordered. Finally, we've confirmed the good condition of the cosmetic surfaces in your new home.

We realize we've covered a lot of information at a time when you have a lot on your mind. What we'd like to do is re-visit your home with you in about 2 months as our warranty procedures describe here in your homeowner manual. At that time, we'll review some of the points we covered today, and of course, answer any questions you may have about using or maintaining your new home.

While we've been thorough in this tour, it's not the same as living in the home. As you get settled and use your home's features on a daily basis, something may fail to function as [Builder] intends it. Our 60-day visit is the appropriate time for you to let us know about items that do not function properly. Of course, in an emergency, please call our office. If an emergency occurs after normal business hours, use the emergency phone numbers located here in your manual and on this sticker. Most homeowners put the emergency phone number sticker on the inside of a cupboard door near the phone.

Do you have any questions? . . .

If you have no further questions, we're finished here for now. Thank you for your time today and thanks again for selecting us as your builder. You have a beautiful home, and I know you'll enjoy it.

- Review procedures for warranty service: emergency and non-emergency. If your company follows the service-oriented procedure of setting an appointment for the first warranty check-up at the orientation, set that appointment with the home buyers at this point (see Chapter 15 for details).
- Ask for questions.
- Thank the home buyers and wish them well in their new home.
- Leave the home, locking the door.

Techniques

Over the years, and through trial and error (lots of error), some techniques that work most of the time have been identified. While such tools may not solve all problems, they help in many cases and are worth learning.

Upon (Early) Arrival. With some buyers "arriving early" means you need to spend the night before the orientation in the home. However, arriving 20 minutes prior to the appointment works most of the time. By arriving early, you are in a position to welcome your home buyers and are also more likely to remain in control of this meeting. While you wait for the buyers to arrive, perform several standard activities:

- Close garage overhead doors.
- Adjust the temperature.
- Assemble the manufacturers' materials.
- Turn on lights.
- Close closet doors.
- Check the home for obvious items.

Have Something to Say in Each Room. Plan at least one agenda item to discuss in each room—switched outlet, adjustable vents, window and screen demonstration, phone and cable TV outlet, smoke alarm, ceiling fan, privacy lock, and so on offer many topics for demonstration and discussion. This approach helps you set the pace of the presentation, retains the home buyers' attention, and keeps everyone together. Explaining most of the home's features in the first room you enter leaves you with little to talk about in the many other empty rooms. Home buyers are likely to separate, wonder off, or become absorbed in minutia in these empty rooms if you are silent.

Hands-On. Where practical throughout this tour, involve your home buyers in a hands-on way. Show them how the windows operate, then ask them to open, close, and lock one. Have them touch the reset button on the disposal and push the test and reset buttons on the ground fault circuit interrupters (GFCI). Have the home buyers participate so they remember the information. Keeping the home buyers physically involved fosters ownership and helps transition them from buying the home to owning the home.

Volunteer Items. Create trust and rapport with home buyers by voluntarily noting missing or incorrect items. This reassures the clients that nothing will be overlooked and establishes you as trustworthy and objective. If you have been fair, it will be easier for you to deny an excessive request. List the following items on the orientation forms:

- Incomplete or missing (powder room cabinet knobs not installed)
- Incorrect (porch light should be polished brass, not antique)
- Dysfunctional (bath fan fails to run)
- Below company standard (mitered corner not smooth at top right of den door, hallway side)
- Damaged (scrape on wall from carpet installation)
- Uncleaned (mud on garage floor, 3' from breaker panel)

Describe the Item. Write a brief description of the item that needs attention rather than the kind of attention to provide. For instance, "MBR door delaminating" not, "replace MBR door." The company chooses the repair method, and you create better raw data for quality analysis. Finding a pattern of defects is easier if you have defect information to study. If all you knew was that the door was replaced, you would have no clue what caused this extra work. Improvement comes from identifying root causes.

Also, avoid descriptions that are general, such as "Clean spots from carpet throughout" or "Touch up paint throughout." Your crews will spend the next 5 years cleaning or painting. Instead, record specifics, "Touch up paint: N LR wall, under front window sill." This may take a bit longer, but you will only do the paint touch-up once. This also gives you control of what the painter touches up rather than putting the responsibility for finding items on the painter.

Follow Through

The worst kept secret in the new home construction industry is that no one really wants to do orientation items. If they are going to get done, someone must do them. The orientation program is a waste of time if the company does not complete the list.

A common element among companies that are successful in completing orientation lists is attention. Have a clear understanding with your trades and employees about the priority of these items and the time frame for completing them. When management makes orientation items a priority, results follow.

Many builders set and meet time frames as short as 10 working days. Only under the most unusual circumstances should an orientation item be left incomplete beyond 30 days. Beyond 30 days, even the most easy-going homeowners become exasperated.

One other important point needs to be emphasized. Completing orientation items means completing all of them—not 19 of 20 or 9 of 11, but all of them. Develop a systematic approach to complete orientation items. To do this, consider these suggestions:

- Notify key trades of the upcoming orientation schedule. Aware of these appointments ahead of time, some will check the home and perform last-minute adjustments. Others will set aside some time, expecting to return.
- Communicate orientation items to the appropriate people immediately and accurately. Notify trades the same day as the orientation or the next business day.
- Phone calls alone are fast but they can open the door to errors, omissions, and a lack of documentation. By copying the original list and highlighting or circling those items for each trade on its copy, everyone will have the same information. Time spent rewriting or typing the list is time wasted; avoid this step with a well-written, legible list.
- Deliver these copies to the trade's mail slot in the construction office, fax it, or drop it in the mail. If the list is faxed, call to confirm receipt of the list. If copies are mailed, phone each trade person to alert him or her that the copy is coming.
- Keep the original list clean and in a safe place. As trades complete their items, they should sign it, date it, copy it, and return it. When the entire list is complete, it should be signed (by the builder and the homeowner), dated, and then filed with all copies attached for reference.
- Each repair performed should be correct and effective; haphazard or half-hearted repairs worsen the original problem.
- Work performed should include clean-up of the work area, including saw dust, bits of wire, or trash. Whether a trade or an in-house employee, everyone who works in a home should finish the job with a check of the area.
- The final task for technicians is notifying the superintendent or whoever is overseeing the work that assigned items have been completed.
- Confirm that the items have been corrected within the required standards. Inspect the items with the superintendent or the person who created the list. Avoid assuming that because you told someone to take care of an item it has been done.
- When you believe all items are complete, check to see what the homeowners think. If any problems exist, the sooner you discover them, the better. Several choices are available for this follow-up: personal visit, phone call, letter, door hanger, e-mail, and so on. A variety of techniques works best because homeowners lifestyles vary.

■ If a homeowner reports that the work performed is unacceptable, inspect it. If the workmanship is below standards, send the trade technician back again. If it is acceptable and within normal standards, think twice before you agree to additional work. Although there is nothing wrong with doing something extra, remember to ask yourself, "Would I be able and willing to provide this for all homeowners?"

14 Predictable Situations

Most home buyers will be delighted with their new homes. They will listen to the information you present, ask several questions, and leave eager to close and move-in. A few will not. Difficult clients will challenge your diplomacy and your patience. As well, your company may occasionally perform at less than its best. Outside circumstances, such as the weather, third parties, or unexpected events in the buyers' lives, can also disrupt the orientation process. This Part is for those situations.

Buyers Arrive with a Ladder and a Flashlight

Whatever super-inspection approach the buyers take, they should find the same level of quality that your company has shown in other homes it has built. They may sit on the floor in the middle of an empty room. Sit down on the floor with them and offer to help look at whatever they are checking. Whatever method the client wants to use can be applied to the showhomes to determine the level of quality to be met.

Buyers Arrive with a List

Acknowledge the clients' list and avoid any appearance of annoyance or intimidation. "I see you've made a list of items. As we go through your home, I'll stop occasionally and ask you to check your list to be certain we talk about everything." Usually such lists include dozens of items that the company addressed during final preparation of the home. Remember your goal is to have the home buyers leave this meeting feeling good about their new home. If they needed to make a list (perhaps because of a bad experience with a previous builder) to achieve that, avoid taking it as an insult and address each item according to your company standards.

Buyers Refuse to Begin Until a Third Party Arrives

The third party can be a real estate agent, relative, or friend. Usually an indication of a lack of trust or self-confidence, the home buyers may feel the orientation rep will put something over on them or that the third party will find items that would otherwise be missed.

Flexibility is the key here. While you wait, offer to look at something noncontroversial. Discuss the main water shut-off in the front yard, the electric meter, or cable TV hookup until the third party arrives. Offer to reschedule. By now, the buyers are feeling more comfortable and may be disappointed that their third party is late. Usually when offered the choice of proceeding or rescheduling, they will decide to go ahead.

Closing Day Inspection

How and when the listed items, if any, will be completed will be uppermost in your buyers' minds. They may ask about damage that might occur during last-minute work. Repair of damage created by work on orientation items is your company's responsibility. In responding to this concern, you essentially have two choices.

Depending on company procedures, you may answer this concern by advising the clients to check their home before bringing in any belongings and if they find any damage to contact the company immediately to request an inspection of that damage. The important point is to establish that the homeowner noted the problem before move-in.

Another option is to schedule a brief visit to the home on the day of closing to confirm completion of items and reassure buyers that no damage occurred during that work. Though time-consuming for all involved, this works well if significant progress on the original (hopefully short) list has been made. To use home buyers' time re-visiting a home and note that only 3 of 18 listed items have been addressed is disrespectful of their time, reinforces the slow response to their list, and can lead to unpleasantness.

One concern with this confirming visit is the possibility that the home buyers will want to create a new list of items; a list can be made on any home. Use common sense. If the hardware technician is still working in the home and another hardware item is noticed, arrange for the item to be corrected. This situation might also be addressed similarly to warranty "add-ons" with the 10-minute rule (see Chapter 16). Certainly cosmetic damage needs to be documented and scheduled for appropriate attention. Minor items might be listed on the 60-day warranty form, which you can start for the home buyers.

Construction Routinely Delivers Incomplete Homes

Some companies think delivering homes with long lists of outstanding items is acceptable or at least unavoidable. These companies limit their success. Homes should be complete when they are delivered. Although a short list of minor items can be tolerated as a result of the orientation process, these items should be completed before the home buyers close and move in.

Delivery of incomplete homes often occurs because quotas are more important than client satisfaction to the company leaders. Other times, builders understand the goal of delivering complete homes, but operationally are out of control. In a few cases, old habits die hard. Some people still believe getting all the last details complete before delivery is impossible. As long as they believe that, they will be unable to meet the goal.

The fact that many companies deliver homes complete—despite tight labor, whimsical weather, seemingly endless client change orders, and unexpected jurisdictional issues—proves it can be done and done with admirable regularity. Once a company commits to this goal, the challenge is developing the systems and habits that make it happen consistently.

Whether company philosophy, operational chaos, antiquated attitudes, or some other reason is behind delivering incomplete homes, your approach to improvement should be the same. Begin by looking for allies. The sales staff is likely to agree with you; a finished product satisfies clients and brings referrals. Sometimes if management hears the same opinion from more than one source, they take the message more seriously. One superintendent may deliver complete homes. Find out what system he or she uses. Can others replicate it?

Next, look for a correlation between delivering complete homes and short warranty lists. Documenting such results can draw attention to the positive impact of finishing the homes and convince the company to make doing so a priority. Use statistics, especially those with dollar signs, and other objective data to make your case calmly. This means using a regular reporting system to show dates, locations, number and nature of orientation items, and time for completion of those items.

Direct quotes from homeowners regarding the condition of their home at move-in can add yet another dimension to your evidence. A homeowner focus group specifically discussing the condition of homes at delivery is another potent approach to getting the attention this area deserves.

Ultimately, if your company is unable or unwilling to make the necessary system adjustments to deliver complete homes, your choices include working in an uncomfortable environment or finding a new job. How can you make this decision? Give your efforts 3 to 6 months. Watch for signs of effort and improvement.

Escrow

To maintain their leverage, some home buyers demand that a portion of their final payment be placed in escrow until all items are complete. Some lenders may impose this requirement as well. If none of the other reasons for delivering complete homes motivates your colleagues, this one should.

Postponing the closing until the items are complete may be a better long-term choice. Escrow funds can lead to a power struggle. The original list of items may be complete but the homeowners now hand the company another list of demands, refusing to release the escrow until this new list is finished. In situations in which escrow funds are unavoidable, your company's best protection is to involve an objective third party who confirms completion of remaining items and releases the balance due.

Familiar Equals Right

Construction offers many right ways of doing things. Your buyer may feel that the way he or she experienced or heard about first is the only right way. Education is the key, supported by your knowledge of how homes are built in your region. "Yes, there are other ways of doing this. We use this one because . . ."

Hidden Agenda

When home buyers have an external reason not to close—for instance, they may be having marital problems or perhaps they found another home they like at a much lower price—they may hide the real issue under a complaint about the home your company built. If home buyers can claim that your company did not fulfill the contract, they can cancel the deal and demand a refund of their deposit. If they cancel the deal for reasons unrelated to your performance under the contract, they will probably lose their deposit, hence their need to "pick a fight" about the home. If your home buyers have such a hidden agenda, the situation will probably need to be settled somewhere other than at the orientation.

Home Inspector's List

Your company standards should meet or exceed all codes and typical industry practices in your region. Judge a home inspector's list according to those standards. Mature builders appreciate such help finding any legitimate items to prevent extra work after home buyers move in. Others resent the inspector's calling attention to items the home buyers might have overlooked.

If the home inspector has an ego-driven need to impress the home buyers or justify the inspection fee, nit-picky items may appear on the inspection report. Calmly and courteously meet your company's normal standards. Address the typical boiler-plate remarks that inspection reports usually contain such as "electrical system could not be fully inspected and may not meet codes" by having copies of three or four inspection reports from different inspection firms. Show the home buyers that these are standard clauses typically included to protect the inspector. Your local building department may help resolve specific questions.

Home Is Not Ready

Any builder can occasionally run into unexpected circumstances that delay delivery. Who has the authority to postpone a closing? Clarify priorities. Do the home buyers have a place to sleep tonight? Is a hotel an option? Where is the moving van full of furniture? How much time is needed to get the home in proper condition?

Balancing these factors requires clear thinking. Focus on solutions. Solve your home buyers' immediate problems first. Then get to work on the cause of the situation. Was this an isolated incident resulting from unique circumstances? Or is it part of a growing pattern? If this failure is a trend, what company operations should be adjusted to prevent a recurrence?

I'm Not Closing Unless . . . .

If clients make closing contingent upon meeting their demands, remain calm. Two possibilities exist. First, the buyers' demands are justified. Second, they are not.

Understand the issue of disagreement. For example, one buyer refused to close because of the quality of exterior paint. He finally revealed his true concern, "Since you need to repaint the house anyway, we'd like to select a different color."

Set the buyer's comments aside and look critically at the painting. Is it within company standards? If so, tell the buyer that and discuss the color issue separately. You might offer to get a price on repainting with a new color through your company. A reminder that landscaping will affect color perception may help. Or, suggest that the buyer consider having the trim color redone to change the appearance—at the buyer's expense, however.

If the paint job is unacceptable, take appropriate steps to correct it. If the paint does need to be completely redone, consider changing the color.

Judging the quality of the paint work and handling the buyer's emotions if you decide the quality is acceptable are both difficult situations.

In any case, try to complete the orientation. "I understand your position. My job here today is to demonstrate the home and list items you have concerns about. I suggest we complete this meeting and then you will have identified all items that need to be resolved so that you can make the decision to close." After all, if there are other issues, finding them all now is the most efficient way to reach a solution and get to closing. If the buyer unreasonably refuses to continue the orientation, that may be a sign that you are dealing with a hidden agenda.

I'm Paying $X for This House

Sometimes a home buyer uses the price of the home to justify a demand. Avoid statements such as "Well, you didn't buy a custom home you know!" or worse, "What'd you expect? This is our cheapest floor plan." Instead say "At half that price, we owe you what we promised. Please show me what you're concerned about."

You might also ask "What was it in our communication with you that make you expect . . . ?" If the client can point to something in the documents that specifies the item in question, or if a reasonable person could have misunderstood what the company promised, you should probably provide it. Then work to correct whatever caused the confusion and prevent a recurrence.

Inclement Weather

Get everyone inside—use the front door—and begin your instructional tour from there. The first item of business after the greeting and introduction is to set a time for performing the exterior portion of the orientation. Yes, this means a second visit. The home buyers do not control the weather any more than you do, and this extra meeting inconveniences them as much as it does you. Each home buyer deserves to hear the entire orientation agenda and confirm the condition of the entire home. Be a good sport about these situations and get the second visit completed within as short a time frame as possible. The same person who is responsible for completing the original interior list should ultimately take responsibility for any exterior items noted at this second visit.

Item Reported by Home Buyers, Not Yet Corrected

One of the more uncomfortable scenarios that can occur at an orientation involves the home buyers recounting how they told their sales person 6 weeks ago about an incorrect detail as all of you stand looking at the incorrect detail during their orientation. A good explanation may exist; the superintendent got the message and the materials needed for the correction have not arrived yet. Here is an opportunity for seamless service. Imagine you arrive at the home already knowing about this and prepared with scheduling information, rather than hearing about it for the first time and knowing nothing about planned corrections.

A less valid explanation is that the sales person assumed the superintendent would notice the problem and correct it without any prompting, so the information never left the sales office. Apologize for the oversight and note the item. Take advantage of this opportunity to do some grooming with the sales person. Ask the superintendent to meet with you and the sales person to review the chain of events and the results. Emphasize the goals of a professional image and satisfied buyers rather than focusing on the error in the sales person's judgment.

Another possible explanation is that the home buyers are mistaken; the home is correct as it is. Even if this turns out to be the case, the issue should have been resolved prior to your meeting with the buyers or, minimally, you should have been informed of their concern. Again, use this as a training opportunity with your colleagues; they may not realize the impact of such details and if you take time to explain, a repetition is less likely.

I Used to Be in Construction

A good response to this claim is "I'm glad to hear that. So many of our buyers do not understand that there are many right ways to build a home. Where was it that you worked in construction?" Lead the conversation around to "This is our way of doing it here."

Latent Expectations

Sometimes buyers realize too late that they wanted some detail different than the way they ordered it. Perhaps they overlooked some aspect of their lifestyle, missed an option you offer, or simply did not think through the plans and specifications clearly enough. In the stress of delivery/closing/moving, they may blame you.

Avoid turning such conversations into arguments. "So, why didn't you order it that way?" or "Didn't you look at the showhome?" are inappropriate responses. "Our construction crews build the home according to the paperwork they receive. We can double check those details if you think we failed to comply with the selection sheets or change orders." This sometimes helps the buyers realize their oversight is not your fault and should not become your problem.

When possible, you might offer to assist them in obtaining the item. For example, if they now wish they had ordered the upgraded microwave or had selected a tub enclosure, you can provide the name and number of the appropriate vendor.

Monthly, Quarterly, or Year-End Crunch

Eager to close homes to meet or beat quotas, some companies shortsightedly push homes to close before they are truly ready. The effects ripple through the entire system, affecting construction, closing, warranty, trades, and ultimately, sales personnel with buyer frustration. The commitment to change this mind set must come from management. Review "Construction Routinely Delivers Incomplete Homes" for suggestions on getting this to change.

Nit-Picking

Differences in standards between the home buyers and their builder are common. This seldom causes a problem when the builder's standards are higher than the home buyers' but does become a concern when the situation is reversed. This is where the benefit of aligning expectations early shows dramatically. If the buyers knew before they committed to purchase the home that this item varied from their personal preference, the issue would have already been resolved. "If it would help, we can visit the showhomes to compare. Our commitment is to build your home to be equivalent to what we advertised. This may be an area where your personal standards are even higher than ours."

Work from a Position of Strength

Denying action on excessive demands is easier if the home is truly ready to deliver. A home in poor condition for delivery stimulates aggressive attitudes with many buyers—even those who are otherwise easy going. You may feel pressure to give extras to compensate the home buyers for your company's lack of good performance. Delivering complete and clean homes eliminates this embarrassment and expense.

Technical Expert

Arrange a meeting with the contractor who did the work if a technical explanation can satisfy the client's concern. Consider the personality of the trade contractor you are thinking of putting in front of your client before scheduling such a meeting. Attend these meetings so you have first-hand knowledge of the conversation and can document any commitment or resolution.

Time Out

"Let's check the rest of the house and come back to this later." Often a minor flaw that catches a home buyer's eye early becomes unimportant after viewing the entire home. Delighted with the overall home, the home buyer is comfortable with accepting a minor imperfection.

Another version of the time-out technique that can work well with items such as carpet seams is to note the buyer's concern and agree to check it at a later date. Some buyers are unable to imagine the empty home with their belongings in it. Once they move in, items buyers thought were catastrophic may not be as big of a concern. The stress of the move has dissipated, furniture is arranged, and the homeowner's perspective is more balanced.

Leave Well-Enough Alone

This approach applies to details such as drywall finish. "I understand why you would notice that in an empty home. My experience has been that we would make it more noticeable if we go over it again." A surprising number of buyers not only understand this concept, but they accept the item and even thank you for the advice.

Noise

Demonstrating a home's features and chatting with the home buyers at orientation is an important task that should be respected by field personnel. Loud activities near the home, such as grading the adjacent lot, are distracting. Make every effort to prevent this. By arriving early for the orientation, you can contact the appropriate people to put such work on temporary hold until the orientation is complete. At the least, keep doors and windows closed to reduce the impact and permit conversation.

No Showhome

Suppose you build custom homes or you do not have showhome to which you can refer? Establishing a common ground for standards is more difficult without sample homes. If another home under construction, viewing that can help. Samples to show style or quality do not always have to come in full-size homes. Pieces of materials to be used, the showrooms of suppliers, a well-organized collection of catalogs, an up-to-date photo album of completed homes (including interior and exterior shots), and the patience to review all of these can assist the builder in influencing home buyers' expectations.

The secret is to arrange for all of this early; the orientation is the time to fulfill expectations—not adjust them. Prevent disagreements with thorough, accurate information. If you do not have showhomes, invest more energy and planning to organize your information.

Something may be overlooked; an item that was not discussed is noticed by the client, who disapproves of the material, method, or quality of the work. When in doubt, error on the side of the home buyer, if at all possible. Your objective is to sell more houses. If a calm explanation doesn't settle the matter, your best choice may be to give in, cheerfully. Arguing for 3 weeks, then giving in means you lose at every juncture; you've spent valuable time "discussing" the matter, ended up repairing the item, and lost the home buyer's good will in the process. Clients remember such battles a long time.

Sales Moves Closing Dates

Some companies allow their sales people to move closing dates up, often in response to pressure from the home buyers or to meet quotas. This is a shortsighted way to do business. This practice may be a sign that the sales team needs training on how to present delivery date policies to clients from the start and how to resist pressure from the home buyers for unrealistic delivery dates.

The construction department may a staunch ally in your campaign to change this practice. Your efforts should follow the points discussed under "Construction Routinely Delivers Incomplete Homes." Use objective information rather than unbridled emotion. Tempting as it is to pound your fist on a table, that will not convince anyone that your view is correct.

This House Isn't Built According to Code

When home buyers claim an item is incorrect based on their understanding of building codes, you really have no argument. "That's not acceptable to us either. Can you give me more information? Which code book are you referring to? Do you have a Part number? We'll see to it everything meets the applicable code."

Time Is Running Out

Occasionally an orientation takes more time than planned because the home buyers ask a lot of questions, because issues about the home arise, or because the orientation began late. This creates a dilemma for an orientation representative who has another appointment.

Scheduling orientations back-to-back with little or no time between them is risky because many unpredictable factors are involved. Calculate the orientation time, driving time from one appointment to the next, time to arrive "early" for the second appointment, and then add a buffer of 30 minutes to be safe. If you find yourself faced with a scheduling problem despite these safeguards, you have several choices.

Excuse yourself and call to arrange for someone else to cover the next appointment.

Contact the clients you are to meet next and see if they are able to change the appointment.

Explain the situation to your current home buyers and set a second appointment to complete their orientation.

Your choice among these responses, or others you think of, will depend on what and who caused the problem. Whatever approach you select, avoid rushing with any client. This can lead to overlooked items and cause debate later.

Triangles

"The salesperson promised . . . ." "Your electrician said he would . . . ." "The painter was going to leave us . . . ." Home buyers may quote a third person who is not present, claiming that a promise was broken or an error was made. Your safest response is to arrange a three-way conversation with this third person, either in person or by phone. If the third person did promise something, in most cases, the client should receive it. Just as often, the home buyer's memory improves when the conversation is recreated. Either way, the matter is settled as far as you are concerned.

Why Don't We Have . . . ?

Avoid the assumption that the buyers are wrong. Although they may be in error, agree willingly to investigate. Keep lines of communication open and friendly.

You may decide to use the question "What was it in our communication with you that made you expect. . . ?" If the home buyers can point to documentation, the company likely owes them the item. More often, this question helps clients realize they made an assumption or they are remembering something another builder mentioned while they were shopping for their new home.

If conversation at the orientation does not clear up this matter, note the issue, describing it as an item to investigate. Avoid recording the item in such a way that the home buyers can claim you committed to providing the item. At this point you are committing only to clear up a misunderstanding. For example, "Investigate: Buyer requests confirmation that carpet pad is correct upgrade. Inspection with installer to be scheduled within 72 hours."

To resolve these situations, go to the original sources to investigate; avoid trusting memory. Begin with the contract, selection sheets, change orders, and company or trade personnel—any document or person who might help clear up the confusion. The final answer is best delivered in a conversation and followed with a written confirmation.

Conducting orientations is a skill that improves with effort and practice. Your greatest assets are knowledge and self-confidence, combined with good communication techniques and thorough preparation. Self-assurance that is communicated to home buyers is not created overnight. With a concerted effort and an organized approach to orientation training, you can excel with this assignment.

Warranty Service

Last, But Not Least

Until recent years, most builders equated customer service with warranty repairs. A more sophisticated home building industry now recognizes that customer service includes everything a company does to, for, or with its clients. As a result of this insight, "complaint department" thinking has been replaced with a recognition that warranty and customer service are not the same thing. Warranty is one part of customer service—a vitally important part—but not all of what makes up a service or a builder's service image.

Because warranty service occurs last in this relationship, the warranty attention that builders provide is remembered and frequently talked about by their homeowners. Stories about how they are treated, the number of service items they have, and the promptness and quality of repairs are just some of the subjects homeowners may describe to other potential buyers.

Unlike the first three client meetings described in this Guide, warranty service is one encounter homeowners would prefer to avoid. The preconstruction conference, frame stage tour, and home buyer orientation each contain elements of anticipation. Many home buyers enjoy the attention. To some extent, the client has control or at least influence over the outcomes of these meetings. Warranty service, however, is different.

Something is wrong with the new home. Repairs may lead to even more inconvenience. Homeowners often resent the fact that decisions about repair methods, the schedule to perform repairs, and the quality of the work are not completely within their control. How can a builder turn all of this potential negativity into something positive?

- Build a good home, one that needs little warranty attention.
- Align the home buyers' expectations regarding their maintenance responsibilities and the company's warranty commitment.
- Complete the home for proper delivery.

Within this context you should experience a minimal number of warranty items. Create an efficient plan for processing those warranty items so you can respond to them swiftly and courteously, and the result will be increased referrals.

Policies and Procedures

Homeowners want all components to perform properly in their new home. Their distant second choice is to have prompt, courteous, and effective warranty service (translation: on-time quality repair work including clean up of the work area and excluding collateral damage). In other words, they want results.

Effective warranty offices focus on procedures that produce results for the homeowners and provide the company with feedback so any recurring items can be eliminated. This means developing habits and systems that aggressively look after clients' interests, generate good records, and communicate with design, purchasing, construction, and sales regarding complaints received from homeowners.

Schedule

In a world with instant messaging, ATMs, overnight delivery, and microwave ovens, it is no wonder homeowners expect prompt service on warranty items. Builders create homes with the support of 35 to 50 individual trade contractors for whom new production creates income but repairing former work does not. It is no wonder that delivering prompt warranty service is an ongoing challenge.

Indeed, the timing of warranty service is not entirely in your control. The homeowners' and the trades' schedules must be coordinated, and if any parts need to be ordered, the process becomes even more complicated.

Control Your Part

You do control some parts of the warranty scheduling process, including acknowledging the homeowner's request, issuing work orders after the inspection, and ensuring that the work ordered is completed.

Track the time from receiving the complaint to making contact to set an inspection appointment. Set your target as a number of hours (not days): 4 hours works well. Be persistent. Avoid the excuse that "I called these homeowners and they never called back so I guess they don't really want this fixed." The only assumption you should make is that your homeowners are busy; keep trying.

Note the date and time of each attempt to reach the homeowner. Leave a message asking that the homeowners call back to set up a time for an inspection, but if you do not hear from them within 48 hours, contact them again. Use a work number, send a fax, or e-mail a request that they call you.

If the second contact does not produce the needed result, mail a letter asking them to contact you. Avoid including the remark, "If I do not hear from you within 10 days I will assume you do not want these items addressed." Such an assumption is usually not accurate and does not release the company from its obligations. Your task remains unchanged: inspect and respond to the list.

The time between your contact and the appointment itself is influenced in part by the homeowner's schedule. However, you should be able to offer homeowners an inspection appointment within 5 business days of your contact with them. If your schedule is so booked that the best you can offer is an appointment 3 weeks into the future, check your time management habits.

If you are organized and efficient, it might be a busy season, and therefore temporary. If the condition is chronic, lasting more than 2 months with no end in sight, staffing level at your company is the next area to be examined. Managers who resist investing in an adequate staff should consider the financial impact of losing sales due to slow warranty service.

Scheduling Inspection Appointments

Many variables can make scheduling back-to-back warranty inspection appointments difficult. However, as you get to know your homeowners and product, you will make increasingly accurate estimates of how long each inspection will take. The following suggestions may help you arrange warranty appointments:

- Depending on the number of items and the personality of the homeowner, you may need from 10 minutes to several hours for each appointment. Be sure to allow a few minutes for casual conversation.
- Allow sufficient time to review and discuss each item, particularly when the homeowner has submitted a list of items you suspect to be home maintenance.
- Listen to everything the homeowner has to say about the items and explain your answers completely; this can save hours of debate later.
- Begin with an estimate of 2 to 3 minutes per item (10 items, allow 20 to 30 minutes) until you get to know the homeowners and become familiar with floor plans and typical items.
- Allow a buffer between appointments, particularly if you will be driving across town to another subdivision. If the meetings are all in the same subdivision, ten minutes is usually sufficient.
- If your company builds in several locations, consider organizing your schedule to visit certain subdivisions on certain days of the week. Think of this plan as a guideline rather than a hard and fast rule.
- To prevent disappointment, make it clear to the homeowner that you are coming to view the items and make a determination regarding what attention is needed, who

should provide that attention, and that any repairs you order will occur in another appointment.

- If you carry tools and perform some repairs, explain this and the subsequent role of trade contractors.
- Immediately record each appointment (including the homeowner's name, subdivision, and phone number) in your appointment book. Call the homeowner 1 or 2 days before the appointment to confirm. They will appreciate your reminder; you will be stood up less often.

Builder-Initiated Appointments

An alternative to waiting for homeowners to initiate the warranty service process is to set the first warranty appointment during the orientation. This practice, which is gaining popularity, offers several benefits.

Clients are less likely to feel as if the company "got our money at closing and then turned their back on us." As a transitional service, this approach is outstanding.

Warranty staff has more control over their schedules because they are initiating the appointment rather than reacting to the homeowner. Surges in sales are automatically leveled out. Homeowners who have a warranty appointment on their calendars are less likely to call the warranty office to report new items (other than emergencies). Rather, they note their concerns and wait for the appointment that's already scheduled.

Because this practice says clearly that the company intends to stand behind its product, most homeowners make more reasonable warranty requests.

The warranty representative, arriving with a preprinted inspection list, establishes him- or herself as the authority on judging whether items in the home meet company standards. The message is "[Builder] wants to confirm that the new home we delivered to you is performing to our standards." This practice makes it easier to deny insignificant items from homeowners.

The small percentage of homeowners who would otherwise not report any warranty items receives attention. Silence does not equate with satisfied. Assuming that no news is good news can mean missed opportunities to create goodwill and stimulate referrals. Few homeowners will bypass attention so graciously offered, and those who do, will at least remember your offer.

Follow-up inspection by a warranty representative encourages construction to get orientation items completed. In fact, review of the work on orientation items could be listed on the checklist.

To implement this procedure, take several steps. Put the procedure into practice and fine-tune your system before you advertise this to home buyers in your homeowner manual.

Appointments. Stop in at the orientation, make introductions, and set the (tentative) appointment. A second choice, if you must miss the orientation, is to call the home buyer, introduce yourself, and set the appointment by phone. The orientation representative should provide the home buyers with your business card and explain that they will hear from you. If the orientation representative and the warranty representative are the same person, setting this appointment is easier.

Inspection Checklist. The second step is to develop an appropriate warranty inspection checklist. An example is shown in Figure 15.1. The homeowners still receive and can use a warranty service request form, such as the one shown in Figure 15.2, to record items they notice or have questions about. In an emergency, they can call for immediate assistance.

Confirmation. A few days before the appointment, call to confirm the date and time. Ask whether the homeowner has noted any items, and if so, request they mail, fax, or e-mail the list for review before the appointment.

This proactive approach can be repeated for the year-end inspection by contacting the homeowner via letter, post card, or phone call during the tenth or eleventh month of their warranty period. The number of items processed at year-end are approximately the same as with traditional systems, but homeowner goodwill increases dramatically.

Prepare

Whether warranty appointments are initiated by your company or in response to contact from the homeowner, research is frequently appropriate before a warranty visit. Remember that you have a wealth of sources to go to for background information, including:

- Sales agreement
- Selection sheets and change orders
- Quality management inspections
- Orientation list
- Warranty document and guidelines
- Previous warranty requests
- Previous inspection reports
- Phone logs
- Correspondence
- Photos or diagrams from previous inspections
- Product specifications
- Manufacturer installation instructions
- Construction personnel
- Sales staff
- Trade contractors
- Manufacturer reps
- Building department inspectors
- Code manuals
- Engineer
- Attorney

Homeowner Manual

An essential tool for warranty inspections is the homeowner manual. Carry it with you and use it to show homeowners the steps they need to take when they have requested "warranty service" on a maintenance item. Rather than say "That's not covered by your warranty," or "We don't fix that, you have to do it," you can say "This is a maintenance item," or "Let's check the manual and see what we're supposed to do with this . . . Okay, here it

FIGURE 15.1 Builder Initiated Warranty Inspection

Name _____ Date _____

Address _____ Community _____

Phone (h) _____ Lot # _____

Phone (w) _____ Plan _____

Email _____ Closing Date _____

_____ ____ 60-Day ____ Year End

- ☐ Backfill
- ☐ Drainage
- ☐ Downspout extensions
- ☐ Concrete flatwork
- ☐ Front Door
  Lock and deadbolt
  Threshold
  Weatherstrip
  Doorbell
- ☐ Back Door
  Lock
  Threshold
  Weatherstrip
- ☐ Patio door lock
- ☐ Garage overhead door
- ☐ Smoke detectors
- ☐ Furnace filter
- ☐ Interior doors
- ☐ Interior trim
- ☐ Cabinets
- ☐ Tile
- ☐ Caulk
- ☐ Window operation
- ☐ Drywall
- ☐ Floor coverings
- ☐ Homeowner list?

By _____

FIGURE 15.2 Warranty Service Request

For your protection and to allow efficient operations, our warranty service system is based on your written report of nonemergency items. Please use this form to notify us of warranty items. Mail to the address shown above. We will contact you to set an inspection appointment. Service appointments are available from 7:00 a.m. to 4:00 p.m., Monday through Friday. Thank you for your cooperation.

Name _____   Date _____

Address _____   Community _____

Ph (Home) _____   Lot # _____

Ph (Work)_____   Plan _____

Ph (Work)_____   Closing Date _____

		Service Action*		
Location	Service Requested	Warranty	Courtesy	Maintenance

*Warranty or Courtesy indicates a [Builder] responsibility. Maintenance indicates a homeowner responsibility.

Comment: _____

_____

_____

Homeowner _____

is. Turns out, this is a maintenance item. I'll be glad to answer any questions you have about taking care of it."

Avoid Prior Conclusions

Although it may be tempting to make conclusions about the warranty visit, resist that trap and wait until you see the items in question. Homeowners often describe items inaccurately or incompletely. Decisions made based on reading their list may not be fair answers. Warranty work, done properly, involves getting out from behind the desk, talking with people, and seeing the homes.

Third Party Support

In some cases, the expertise of a trade contractor, manufacturer's representative, or building department official may help you convince a homeowner that the material used or workmanship applied is proper. At the same time, expert support might help you determine that attention is in order. Either way, if you believe this support is appropriate, arrange to have that third person attend the first appointment, if possible. Homeowners resent repetitious appointments to inspect the same item, and so should you.

Avoid sending third parties to inspect items without attending yourself. You only need to have one conversation with a homeowner who says, "The carpet rep said the carpet needs to be replaced" when the written report from that representative says, "The homeowner needs to vacuum more frequently." to understand why. Unfortunately, many warranty representatives have had to learn this lesson the hard way.

Conduct

Be on time for the warranty appointment. If you have not met the homeowner(s) before, introduce yourself and provide your business card. Take a few moments to chat and get to know them. The insights you gain into their personalities and priorities can help you attend to their items more effectively.

Inspect the items listed in as logical an order as possible. Adapting the itinerary of the frame stage tour and orientation works well. Begin with exterior items, if any, move next to interior items, and end in the kitchen.

Frequently you can make inspection notes directly on the warranty request form (Figure 15.2) or your company warranty checklist (see Figure 15.1). If the number of items or the manner in which the homeowner filled out the warranty service request make this impractical, have a separate inspection form similar to the one shown in Figure 15.3 ready for your notes. Some companies are now using handheld computers for this process. Until that is more common, remember to always have a pen and notepad when you meet with a client, even if you are addressing only one item.

Where appropriate, add photos (especially useful with drainage problems), diagrams, and direct quotes from the homeowner to your inspection notes. Also, list follow-up tasks you intend to perform, such as writing a confirming letter or any additional research. Sign and date all pages of your notes from inspections.

FIGURE 15.3 Warranty Inspection

Day _____ Date _____ Time _____

Community _____ Lot#_____ Plan _____

Homeowner _____ Closing Date _____

Address _____

Phone (h) _____ (w) _____

Item	Action	Work Order #

Notes

_____

_____

_____

_____

_____

_____

By _____

Conclude the visit by explaining what will happen next. Describe the repair process so the homeowner will know what to expect. If any issues are unresolved, set a time for an update (and note it on your calendar). Contact the homeowners on time even if it is to tell them you have nothing to tell them—yet. Set another time for an update.

If your company uses the "work date" approach for repair appointments, ask the homeowner for a date (usually at least 10 business days into the future) when access to the home can be arranged. Record this date in your inspection notes so the information is accurately passed along to the trades involved.

Follow Through

Ideally, you get work orders issued to trades or in-house technicians within 1 work day of the inspection. A sample work order appears in Figure 15.4. The timing of this administrative detail significantly influences the total amount of time from report to repair. (Imagine downloading the results of your inspection into the main database and forwarding the repair details immediately to trades.)

Do your part by ensuring that the work order you issue contains all needed information. Put yourself in the place of the person performing the repair and anticipate the details he or she will need to know.

If the work should be paid for by your company, make that commitment clear when you communicate to the trade. In most cases, you will want to get a price on the work unless standardized pricing has been established.

Traditionally builders used a 30-day time frame for warranty items. Because customer satisfaction has been emphasized and some businesses have responded more quickly than in the past, builders have become more aggressive in this area. Ten work days is the goal, and many companies are staying within that time frame. To do this, establish a routine time to update your records and review outstanding work orders.

If you denied any requested service items, make certain these too are documented, either on a copy of the original list that you left with the homeowner, or for more significant items, in a letter that confirmed the answer you gave in conversation. Several examples of letters denying action in a variety of situations can be found in the Home Builder Press publication by Carol Smith, *Dear Homeowner.*

Enforcing Time Frames

One of the most effective steps you can take to provide homeowners with better service is to check on warranty items before they get old. When you routinely enforce time frames, the attitude, "If they really wanted it done, someone would have called us" is replaced with "Let's get this scheduled. You know we'll hear from [Builder] if we don't get this taken care of." This shift in attitude improves service significantly. Many trades perform to the level you set, so make your position on this issue clear from the beginning.

For most companies, weekly review of warranty work orders serves two purposes. Work orders are promptly investigated. Contact the homeowners to let them know you are checking on the status of the work ordered because your records show it remains incomplete. On some occasions, you may discover the work is complete and the confirmation has not yet reached your office. If the work is incomplete, your follow up reassures the homeowner, and you can confirm the information with the trade.

FIGURE 15.4 Sample Warranty Work Order

Date _____ Community _____

Work Order # _____ Lot # _____

Purchase Order # _____ Floor Plan _____

Contractor _____ Homeowner _____

Address _____ Address _____

Phone _____ Phone _____

Work requested:

Requested by:

Comment on work performed:

The homeowner has received a copy of this service order and will expect this work to be completed within 10 business days. It is your responsibility to set a service appointment although the homeowner may call you to expedite this. Upon completion of the work, sign and return this form for the warranty file. Your attention and cooperation are appreciated!

Completed by _____ Date _____

Homeowner _____ Date _____

Also, routine analysis of warranty work identifies recurring items. Once you are aware of a problem, you can often eliminate it. The secret to success is constant attention.

Tracking Items

Whether your warranty process is supported by computer software or you use a manual system, develop relevant reports. This means tracking warranty items, not "letters" or "calls."

For analysis of warranty work to stimulate improvement, details are essential. Knowing that your warranty office is addressing "48 letters" does not tell you whether the problems are cabinet, window, plumbing, or drywall. Identifying specific quality issues is impossible unless you look into the details. Likewise, identifying unresponsive trades is more difficult if all you know is that you have 19 "old" lists. You need to know which trades are causing service delays and that means tracking items.

Computer Support. With typical computer-supported systems, a report lists each address, the trade needed, and a brief description of the item(s) that trade has been asked to correct. This data can usually be sorted by trade, homeowner, subdivision, and range of dates.

As information becomes available, warranty personnel make notes on these printed reports. On a routine day, usually the day before the weekly warranty staff meeting, these notes are used to update the next printed report; completed items are removed and saved to permanent records for the home involved. The updated report is printed, and the cycle begins again.

As data accumulates in the system, reports based on floor plan, individual trades or particular homeowners, specific subdivisions, or a range of dates—among other sort criteria—should be available.

Manual Systems. If your company is still looking for that perfect warranty management software, a workable manual system can be set up.

- Create a work order binder with an index tab for each trade that routinely receives work orders.
- Each Part in the binder should contain a log like the one in Figure 15.5
- Log new work orders and add them at the front of existing work orders, so the oldest work orders are at the back.
- Daily or weekly, depending on volume of work, note the completion date of each returned (signed) work order on the work order log.
- Match the completed work orders to the copy in the binder and remove the copy from the binder.
- File the signed copy in the home's warranty file. Dispose of the office binder copy unless it contains relevant notes, in which case file that copy as well.
- You can fax the work order log to trades as an informal summary of outstanding work orders. They can compare what their records show and stay on track.

What remains in the updated binder is your outstanding work. Beginning at the back of each Part, check for work orders that are approaching their expiration dates. Call the tardy trade and the affected homeowner to explain the delay and get the process moving again. If a valid reason exists for work being incomplete, such as the homeowner is enjoy-

FIGURE 15.5 Sample Work Order Log

Contractor _____

Phone _____

Date Issued	Completion Date	Work Order #	Homeowners	Actual Completion	# of Days

ing a cruise, the work order should be placed on hold in a tickler file and reactivated at an appropriate date.

If there are just a few work orders, put pending work orders on a bulletin board. A quick glance identifies any that require your intervention. When work is completed, remove and file them.

Anyone who comes into the office can readily see the amount of warranty work waiting to be performed. This can be an advantage or a disadvantage depending on who's doing the looking. The plumber who has two "old" service orders may point to an expired order for the cabinet company and use their slow performance to defend his own (the "everybody's doing it" defense).

Whatever your system, constant attention is essential for results. If you wait until monthly reports are compiled, circulated, reviewed, and acted upon, the homeowners may be picketing before anything changes. Monthly reports provide useful long-term views and the raw material for in-depth analysis. They help identify recurring concerns and track the results of improvement efforts. However, the daily or weekly follow-up attention is what produces results for waiting homeowners.

Closure

Follow through brings each warranty item to closure. Closure means that the company, the homeowner, and the warranty file all agree the builder has taken care of the problem. Every item listed by a homeowner on a service request should be responded to and that response should be documented. If the homeowner reported 14 items, you need to document 14 responses, whether those responses are yes or no.

Confirm Satisfaction

An important element in follow through is checking on satisfaction with your homeowners. The quickest method to do this is to visit or call and ask them.

In as many cases as possible, contact the homeowners in person or by phone to confirm that the issue was resolved. Especially on the more significant issues, such as no heat, major drywall repairs, or carpet replacement, a call to confirm the work is complete is essential.

If the homeowner is dissatisfied, it is far better for you to hear about it than the homeowner's neighbors or friends. If the homeowner reports that work is complete but unacceptable, set an inspection appointment and review the item in question. Complaints about the quality of repair work cannot be resolved from behind a desk.

If the results of your follow up are less than pleasing, what you need is a plan of attack, not a hiding place. Expect that some items will need secondary attention such as sending the trade back, visiting the home to check on quality of repairs, or ordering a more extensive repair because the first effort was unsuccessful in meeting company standards.

Monitor the number of items that come across the warranty desk a second (or even a third) time. Ask the question, item by item, "Why was this item not resolved?" If you can identify common causes you may be able to eliminate some of them.

16 Predictable Situations

Performing warranty service for homeowners provides a variety of experiences, ranging from funny to frustrating, from gratifying to outrageous. Those that follow are fairly common, but one word of caution—avoid saying "Now I've heard it all" because within a short time, these words will haunt you.

Access

Arranging access to homes for inspection or repairs requires persistence and determination. Challenges stem from the fact that most homeowners are extremely busy while others turn appointment setting into a power struggle. Your goal is the same regardless: respond to reported items.

Keys or Appointments?

Many builders today prefer to have an adult present during any interior warranty inspection or repair work. Should this be the position your company takes, alert homeowners to this early by including the information in your homeowner manual. The *Homeowner Manual Template* offers this paragraph on the subject:

[Builder] conducts inspections of interior warranty items only when an adult is available to accompany our representative and point out the items you have listed. Both our in-house service technicians and those of our trade contractors will likewise perform repairs only when an adult is available to admit them to your home. An adult is a person 18 or older who has your authorization to admit service personnel and sign completed work orders.

We do not accept keys, nor will we permit our trade contractors to accept a key and work in your home without an adult present. While we recognize that this means processing warranty service items may take longer, we believe your peace of mind and security should be our first concern.

Key Release

If your company accepts keys to work in homes when no adult is present, recognize that no release, waiver, disclaimer, or agreement of any kind, regardless of how many of your attorneys work on the wording will protect your organization from responsibility and liability if problems occur. Proceed with great care and treat homeowner keys with the same or even greater care than you do your house keys.

Homeowner Temporarily Unavailable

If your homeowner is about to go on vacation, have relatives visit for a month, start a demanding new job, or for any other reason prefers not to have warranty repairs performed right now, put the work on hold. This is the traditionally accepted step under such circumstances.

The traditional mistake is to put responsibility on the homeowner to reactivate this work. The result is usually an angry call 6 weeks later from the homeowner, asking when this work will be completed. Avoid this by noting the hold on your calendar, 2 to 4 weeks out, and check in with your homeowners to see if they are ready to set repair appointments. If the warranty period is nearing its expiration, you can limit the hold to between 10 and 30 days.

Additional Items

The homeowner has faxed a list of items to you; you set an appointment to inspect them. During the appointment, the homeowner mentions that he has noticed three additional things he'd like you to review. Simply say "Of course. What are they?" Inspect the items and record each along with your response in your inspection notes. This is one of the reasons you included a time buffer between scheduled appointments.

New items pointed out by the homeowner while technicians are working in the home can be screened with the "10-minute rule." With this policy, the technician corrects these new items if he or she agrees that the items are covered by the warranty, and they can be completed within 10 minutes (or some other amount of time you select). The technician should note all additional items completed on the original work order so the warranty file is complete. If technicians are not qualified to decide whether an item is covered by the warranty, they probably need more training.

Items that take longer than 10 minutes to correct, require special parts, or are questionable as to warranty coverage should be directed through the warranty reporting process. This common sense approach is reasonable to homeowners and avoids inefficiencies for everyone.

Alternative Dispute Resolution

In the regrettable event that a warranty disagreement cannot be resolved between your company and the homeowner, having an alternative dispute resolution clause as part of the warranty document can forestall litigation, which saves everyone time and money. The warranty might include a clause such as the one that follows:

Alternative Dispute Resolution

The Owner shall promptly contact the Company's warranty department regarding any disputes involving this Agreement. If discussions between the parties do not resolve such dispute, either party may, upon written notice to the other party, submit such dispute to arbitration with each party hereto selecting one arbitrator, who shall then select the third arbitrator. The arbitrators shall proceed under the construction industry rules of the American Arbitration Association. The award of the majority of the arbitrators shall be final, conclusive, and binding upon the parties. The expenses of the arbitrators shall be shared equally, but each party shall bear its own fees and costs.

To use arbitration effectively to settle a dispute, be prepared to present your company's side of the issue.

- Organize the file in chronologic order.
- Read all of it.
- Restrain your emotions and ask what you can prove. (This is one reason to do all that documentation.)
- Obtain and document historical background from other personnel.
- Confirm that all work orders issued are accounted for and their status known.
- Add copies of applicable manufacturer warranties to the file.
- Alert involved personnel and trades, confirming the arbitration date and their availability to attend.
- Meet with these participants to discuss the events that led to the disagreement and anticipate points that the opposing side might raise in the arbitration.

Angry Letter

An angry homeowner letter can appear on the desk of any warranty representative. This does not make you a bad person, but the way you respond can show how professional you are. Keep these suggestions in mind.

- Read the letter, withholding comments. Think whatever you want, but say nothing.
- Make a copy to work from, file the original with no notes on it.
- Put the copy of the letter aside until the next work day. Allow your natural (and sometimes appropriate) defensiveness, frustration, and anger to subside.
- The next day, re-read the letter and identify each issue, sifting out the homeowner's emotional comments.
- Categorize and prioritize the issues.
- Check the file for background information on each issue.
- Talk to others who may add to what you learn from the file.
- Set an appointment with the homeowner to inspect the items.
- Come to conclusions based on the facts you gather and fair consideration of all circumstances.
- Follow through with appropriate actions. Issue work orders or send a letter confirming denial of requested service.
- Check the big picture. Did any of the company systems upset the homeowner?

- Implement improvements to company systems, as needed. Candidates include product design, purchasing decisions, construction scheduling and supervision, trade performance, and staff training

Consumer Protection Entities

Occasionally homeowners skip communicating to you and complain directly to the Better Business Bureau, Office of Consumer Affairs, Attorney General, Licensing Board, or some similar consumer protection entity about items that they never reported to you. When this occurs, the following steps may help.

Double check previous letters and inspections for any mention of their complaints. Then contact the homeowner as follows: "Mrs. Jones, I have received a copy of your letter to the <consumer protection entity>. I've checked your file and found no previous notice about these items. When did you first send this list to us?"

Regardless of the answer continue with "I apologize. We do not have your letter. If we had received it, you would have heard from us. Let's set an inspection appointment and get busy on these items."

Inspect the items and order approved work to be performed according to your normal standards and procedures.

After completion of the approved work, call to Mrs. Jones: "Mrs. Jones, I just wanted to confirm the information I have here that your April 27 list has been completed. Again, I apologize that we somehow did not get your original letter. If you contact us again and do not get a response within 3 days, please call me. It's faster for you to work directly with us than to go through the <consumer protection entity>."

Update the consumer protection entity about your actions to resolve this matter.

Cosmetic Damage

Nearly every builder orientation form includes a statement limiting the builder's responsibility for repairs of surface damage reported after the homeowners move in. The concept behind this is reasonable. Builders want no liability for these expensive repairs once the homeowners have control of how the home's surfaces are treated.

Although the logic seems fair, the reality is complicated. At the orientation, typically three or more adults tour a clean, empty home in broad daylight, with the purpose—among others—of confirming the condition of cosmetic surfaces. Although the likelihood of overlooking significant surface damage is low, it can happen. More common than that, however, is cosmetic damage that appears after homeowners move in and they have not caused it.

Understandably, homeowners are emotional about these situations. Equally as understandable is the confusion in the minds of front-line personnel who are too often taught only to apply black and white standards, policies, and procedures. This education is the starting point; warranty personnel also need training and guidance in making judgment calls.

To be fair to homeowners, each situation must be evaluated on its own merits. Avoid winning on a technicality. "You signed the orientation form so this repair is your problem" is likely to destroy client goodwill. Minimally, you owe the homeowners an opportunity to show you what they are talking about and explain their point of view.

Consider this example. If the electrician drops a tool into the tub during construction and is relieved to see no damage had occurred, he may leave behind a crack that is invisible to the eye. After move in, when the homeowner uses the tub, the weight and temperature of water causes the chip to appear.

Establishing guidelines for untangling these situations can help. Think of these as "back door standards," guidelines for decisions that are not published to clients but they provide some boundaries for your discretionary decisions. These guidelines might be developed based on a combination of the following criteria:

- Number of days
- Amount of money
- Specific items or type of repair

For example, if a homeowner discovers a cut in the vinyl in the corner of the laundry room—one that your inspection suggests probably happened during installation of the floor covering itself—you should repair it. If the vinyl has a 6-inch long, 2-inch wide rip in front of the leg of the washing machine that the homeowners moved, give them the phone number of the people who can do the repair.

Your back door standards might provide you with the latitude to any of the following:

- Repair any cosmetic damage discovered during the first 5 days.
- Spend up to $100 for cosmetic repairs at any time.
- Replace any window that gets a stress crack.
- Offer a patch or surface repair for any countertop, resilient floor, tub, or sink. If the homeowner insists on a replacement of the item, provide the appropriate names and numbers for them to arrange and pay for this on their own.

Warranty service cannot be managed from a book of printed standards regardless of the author, size, or level of detail. You begin with knowledge of such standards, and you must listen and think, too.

Defective Material

A sinking feeling comes with the realization that your company installed defective materials in a number of homes. Having a framework for analysis and response can ease your discomfort. Recognize that material defects can result from the following:

- Flaws in the component's design—all of the product can show defects.
- One batch of the product turns out to be defective.
- Installation errors. (When all else fails, read the directions?)
- Improper maintenance by the homeowner.

To minimize such catastrophes:

- Select components with long-term performance in mind.
- Conduct research to learn about the product.
- Avoid basing purchasing decisions solely on cost; saving a little now can cost a fortune later.
- Review manufacturer installation instructions in detail and follow them. This means training installation crews.

- Consider having a manufacturer representative inspect installation and sign off on the work until crews are proficient.
- Maintain accurate and complete files so you can determine what materials you used where. Include appropriate maintenance information in your homeowner manual.

If, despite your company's best efforts, the worst happens, some guidelines may lessen your feeling of helplessness.

- Treat the matter with the utmost urgency—as your homeowners will.
- Immediately begin investigating. Designate one person to oversee the investigation to avoid confusion and duplication of effort.
- Schedule regular updates for involved staff.
- Define the problem, identify possible responses, and determine who is responsible or who might contribute to solutions.
- How many homes are affected? What is their present condition?
- Keep accurate records of conversations with manufacturers and suppliers, including the name of anyone you spoke to, the date, and key points of the conversation.
- Follow through on any commitments you make to supply manufacturers and others with information. Cooperate with necessary and appropriate inspections.
- Avoid appearing to shirk all responsibility for the problem. At the least, you owe your homeowners guidance and informational support.
- Promptly alert your insurance company and your attorney. If you do not have an attorney, this is a good time to get one.
- Keep in touch with everyone, especially affected homeowners. Provide factual information you are certain is correct and realistic a time frame for resolution, taking into account factors outside your control.
- Avoid group meetings with large numbers of angry people. Communicate with homeowners individually, by phone and letter.
- Check with other builders who may have used the same product.
- Consult with your home builders association and the National Association of Home Builders Research Center (800-638-8556).

Whatever the outcome of your investigation, follow through meticulously and document all work performed under your authority. Imagine your successor, 3 years from now, looking in a file to determine how to respond to a subsequent homeowner with a concern. What information should be there?

Difference in Standards

Despite showhomes, detailed paperwork, and good communication, sometimes a homeowner wants quality higher than what your company promised or perhaps higher than what is physically possible by any builder at any price. Such discussions frequently involve subjective or cosmetic aspects of the home for which no measurable standards exist.

In conversations with homeowners over such topics, take the approach "Your standards are even higher than ours. My job is to make certain we delivered everything we sold you. If you want to make it even better, I will be happy to assist with whatever information I have available." In a follow up, confirming letter, the paragraph below may be useful:

While I recognize that some of your personal standards exceed <Builder> standards, these standards were included in the terms of our agreement with you at the time our contract was signed. Our intention is to fulfill our obligations as defined by these documents.

Drama

Some homeowners become so angry with their builder they are willing to diminish the value of their property (and that of neighbors) by announcing to the world "This is a bad house. Talk to me before buying from [Builder]." They want to damage your company's business; they are willing to damage their investment to accomplish this.

Begin with the direct approach. Confront your homeowner. "Mrs. Jones, I see by the search light and hot air balloons in your front yard that you are unhappy with something. This is not good for us or for your property value. Can we discuss it?" Recognize you may give in on something to resolve this and go prepared with some options in mind. Work hard to be objective; the company may have made unfair or insensitive decisions that need to be reconsidered.

Listen, and fully investigate your client's issues promptly. Stay in touch while conducting research. Fully explain denied items using the "soft no" or the "terminal no" as described in Chapter 7. Both techniques help you avoid sounding rude or uncaring, arbitrary or inflexible. Be friendly and caring. Document all issues and responses.

If your investigation shows that the homeowner is demanding something impossible to deliver, a conversation with your company attorney might be your last resort.

Extended Hours

With more businesses offering near 24/7 access, the fact that homeowners expect service outside traditional work hours is no surprise.

"Off hours" appointments are difficult to manage due to factors unique to home building. Highlight these for clients in your homeowner manual. The wording suggested in the *Homeowner Manual Template* can help.

Inspection and Work Hours

Many homeowners ask whether evening and weekend appointment times are available. [Builder] understands the desire for appointments outside normal business hours. We recognize the trend to services being available "24/7" in many businesses. However, in investigating how such appointments could be arranged, we discovered many factors that make extended service hours impractical.

1. A significant portion of repairs require daylight for proper execution. This applies to drywall, paint, and exterior work of almost any type.
2. We also found that most of the 35 to 50 independent trade contractors who helped us build your home—many of whom operate as small companies—were unable to work all week and also be available for extended hours. Therefore, the few repairs that could be performed in off-hours failed to eliminate the need for repair appointments during normal hours.

3. Administrative staff and supervisors would need to be available to answer questions. Having some personnel work extended hours meant being short staffed during normal business hours.
4. When we calculated the impact on wages and salaries for adding more personnel or compensating existing personnel for working non-traditional hours, we found that this affected overhead, and consequently the prices of our homes.

We are still looking for a workable long-term answer to this recognized dilemma. Meanwhile, our warranty hours will be as follows:

Administrative staff:	Monday through Friday, 8 a.m. until 5 p.m.
Inspection appointments:	Monday through Friday, 7 a.m. until 4 p.m.
Work appointments:	Monday through Friday, 7 a.m. until 4 p.m.

Evening and weekend appointments are reserved for emergency situations. We appreciate your understanding and cooperation with these policies.

Note that if a trade has missed a repair appointment (usually when your homeowner took a vacation day for the visit), a more aggressive attitude on your part on behalf of the homeowner is justified. Insisting on an "off hours" appointment that is less inconvenient to the homeowner may help the trade to remember future warranty appointments.

Exterior Work

Although your company may not require that a homeowner be present during exterior repair work, make it a habit to inform the homeowner when such work will take place. Instruct the technician to leave a door hanger or some other documentation to confirm he or she was on the property.

Homeowner's Possessions

When an Atlanta builder agreed to resurface a hardwood floor, the next topic of discussion was who would move the homeowners' expensive entertainment system out of the family room. Resolution came when the builder offered the homeowners a choice between moving the entertainment system or receiving a check for the cost of the floor work, and then arranging the work on their own. The homeowners agreed to move the entertainment system.

This disagreement, which lasted several weeks, would have been easier to resolve if the builder's position on personal belongings had been clear from the beginning. To accomplish this, you may want to use this Homeowner Manual Template paragraph in the company homeowner manual:

In all work that we perform for our homeowners we are concerned that their personal belongings be protected. When warranty work is needed in your home, we ask that you remove vulnerable items or items that might make performing the repair difficult. [Builder] and trade personnel will reschedule a repair appointment rather than risk damaging your belongings.

I Didn't Buy a Patched House

This statement is a demand that a component (countertop, bathtub, or resilient floor, for example) be replaced rather than repaired. It is one of the more difficult homeowner remarks for front-line warranty personnel to respond to.

The fact is that every home contains patches. However, pointing this out to an upset homeowner may not help much. Instead, try to understand the homeowner's concern. Usually one of three possibilities will apply: cosmetic, practical, or psychological. The homeowner may be worried that the repair will:

- Be noticeable and unattractive.
- Last only long enough for the warranty to expire and then cause the homeowner repair expense.
- Destroy the newness of the home, making it "damaged goods."

Combinations of these objections are also possible. Once you know which you are dealing with, address the underlying concern(s).

Cosmetic

In response to cosmetic concerns, ensure the homeowner that the repair you are offering has been performed successfully many times. Offer to inspect the completed work to confirm that the result meets company standards.

In such follow-up inspections, apply reasonable criteria. For instance, supposing you order a patch for a vinyl floor. If the repair draws your eye upon entering the room or can be easily noticed from any position, standing or sitting, replace the vinyl. If the repair can be seen only while you are on your hands and knees, as when cleaning the floor, it is acceptable. If the floor needs five such repairs and the probable cause is construction damage that went unnoticed at the orientation (you will suspect this when such damage is common in the subdivision), replace the floor covering. Then work on getting construction personnel to protect surfaces more effectively.

Practical

If practical concerns are the problem, offer a letter extending the warranty on this one item for an additional year. This shows your confidence in the quality of the repair work you are offering.

Psychological

The psychological concern is often the most difficult to resolve. The client may be unable to articulate what is uncomfortable. Combining both solutions described above may soothe the homeowner's sense that the home is no longer new. If this is not acceptable you are faced with an image level judgment call (see Chapter 7 for more suggestions on judgment calls).

I Don't Care What Your Manual Says

In addition to the hints under "Difference in Standards" you might get good results from asking this homeowner "What was it in our communications with you that made you expect . . . ?"

If the homeowner can point to documentation that can reasonably be interpreted to mean what the homeowner believes it means, you probably should provide the item. You may want to revise the document to prevent a recurrence of the misunderstanding. However, recognize that sometimes homeowners' expectations exceed all reasonable interpretations of your company's commitments. In such cases, your choices are limited to giving in to unfair demands or having a disgruntled client. Pleasing one hundred percent of your clients one hundred percent of the time is unlikely.

I Paid $X for This House

Avoid knee jerk reactions such as "Well, you did not buy a custom home you know!" or worse "This is our least cheapest model." Instead say "At half that price, we owe you what we promised." Ask what in the process made the client believe he or she had something different in the home. Again, if a reasonable person could have misunderstood what was promised, go into recovery mode and provide the needed attention. Then fine-tune documents and systems to prevent a recurrence of the misunderstanding.

I've Already Talked to My Attorney

Nearly everyone has an attorney or at least knows this threat can produce results. Faced with this or similar comments from a homeowner, review all facts and circumstances. If you believe you are on firm ground, keep lines of communication open and make it clear that the threat will not change your response.

"I regret that you feel that way. I understand that you have to do what you believe to be right. I'll be happy to review the details with you if that would help. Please be sure your attorney has copies of your contract with us as well as the warranty. We intend to fulfill the terms of these documents."

If your company receives correspondence from a homeowner's attorney, seek help from your company's attorney. Avoid carrying on conversations or correspondence with an attorney without guidance from your attorney. You can inadvertently say something that compromises your company's otherwise legitimate defense.

I Want a Copy of Everything in the Warranty File

Copies of the contents of a warranty file belong to the company and should be shared only with the current owner of the home in question. The request for copies of the entire file often comes from a listing real estate agent who may mention "disclosure laws" to get your attention. However, disclosure is the obligation of the seller (your original homeowners) and does not apply to your company under these circumstances.

Remember to be courteous to all parties (because this real estate agent may sell one of your new homes in the future). Explain that company policy protects the privacy of the homeowner of record and that you can provide information upon receipt of a written request from the current homeowner, who, you can suggest, probably already has all this information.

I Want to Talk to the Owner

As with some of the other threatening comments homeowners may make, avoid appearing intimidated. Respond calmly and courteously. "You are always welcome to do so. One thing I'd point out to you, however, is that I am working within the guidelines the owner has given me."

Whether, as a general practice, you follow this conversation by alerting your company owner is a matter for you to discuss with the owner. Some company owners prefer advanced notice; others want to be able to say with complete honestly "This is the first I've heard about this. I appreciate your bringing the matter to our attention and we'll reconsider your situation. We'll get back to you by Thursday." Refer to "Going Over Your Head" for more suggestions.

Legal Action Pending

When a homeowner initiates legal action, many companies mistakenly take the position of putting all pending warranty work on "hold" until the legal proceedings are resolved. This question may end up being academic because the homeowner will refuse access to the home. If possible, however, the company should complete warranty work that has been approved and ordered so far. This minimizes the number of items under discussion in legal proceedings and shows good faith on the part of the company.

Listing Agent List

Listing agents sometimes become so excited about their work they feel everyone else should treat their needs with the same urgency they do. ("I need you to replace the driveway, plants two more trees, and have the carpet cleaned by Thursday so I can show the property.") Show consistent courtesy and respect, explain normal reporting procedures by saying, "I'll be happy to help you. Here's what we need to do. . . . ," and describe the reporting procedure that will initiate an inspection.

Frequently the list of items the agent expects your company to address includes a considerable number of maintenance tasks the homeowner has ignored. Inspect and make warranty judgement calls based on normal company guidelines and policies. Maintenance is the homeowners' responsibility even if they are listing their home for sale.

Media

Remember nothing is ever off the record with a reporter. Keeping secrets goes against their nature and sense of journalistic professionalism. Comments made off the record are likely to appear, credited to "a high ranking official" or "a source revealed."

In addition to eking out information, reporters are also interested in selling papers or achieving ratings. Sometimes they might apply a slightly different perspective to a story to heighten interest in it.

In one example, a reporter talked with a builder-developer who was embroiled in a disagreement with a no-growth group. The reporter asked whether engineering for a new project was complete. The developer responded that engineering was in progress and would be completed in 1 to 2 weeks. The resulting story stated "The developer admitted the required engineering had not been done." The impression created was quite different from what was actually happening, but made a more intriguing story.

Rather than say something that could be taken out of context to create a different meaning, explain in a friendly and cooperative tone that you "do not have all the facts and do not want to give out incorrect information. The person to speak to is . . . ." and provide the name of your company's designated media representative.

As shown in the example, even this person can be misquoted. The ideal approach, when possible, is to obtain a written list of questions and a deadline, then provide written responses. This principle also applies in an emergency situation such as an accident on the job site.

Avoid going to the other extreme, screaming "No comment" and slamming a door in the face of the reporter. Think about your reaction when a news magazine program attempts to interview the opposing side and someone spits on the camera lens. Your conclusion is likely to be that he or she is guilty, as well as rude.

If the company can show itself to be a reasonable and caring organization that operates in a reputable manner, a disagreement with a client makes a dull story and is likely to get little attention.

Method of Repair

Homeowners may demand that you use their repair methods or that you replace an item when a repair is appropriate. While you should certainly listen carefully to the reasons that homeowners give and suggestions they make, be cautious about using unfamiliar repair procedures or those you know have not worked well in the past. Following the dictates of the homeowner may seem on the surface to be service oriented, but when problems develop as a result, any benefits are lost.

Likewise, be cautious about replacing an item that can successfully be repaired. The following letter, borrowed from *Dear Homeowner* might be of use in such situations.

In response to your request, work order # _____ was issued on <date>.

The work order provides for repair of an interior door that has delaminated. This repair has been performed in the past with excellent results.

Although the choice of a method of repair is specifically the company's by the terms of the warranty, you have the option taking responsibility for correcting the item at your own expense and using a method of your choice. If you decide to proceed with another method of repair, simply inform the service technician or trade contractor and we will cancel the work order and consider this matter resolved.

The service technician or trade contractor assigned to complete this work will contact you during the next several days to arrange an appointment during normal service hours (8:00 a.m. to 4:00 p.m., Monday through Friday).

Please call me if you to discuss this if you have any concerns about the intended work or our procedures.

Missed Appointments

Alert homeowners that missed appointments are an acknowledged part of warranty work. You can include this paragraph from the *Homeowner Manual Template* in your manual as a way to introduce this subject:

> Good communication is one key to successful completion of warranty items. We strive to keep homeowners informed and to protect them from inconvenience. One of our challenges in this regard is when unexpected events sometimes result in missed appointments.
>
> If a [Builder] employee or a trade person will be late, he or she should contact you as soon as the delay is recognized, offering you a choice of a later time the same day or a completely different appointment. If you must miss an appointment, we appreciate being alerted as soon as you realize your schedule has changed. We can put work orders on "hold" for 10 to 30 days and re-activate them when your schedule offers a better opportunity to arrange access to the home.

If the homeowner misses the appointment give him or her a second and perhaps even a third chance. Use confirming calls to prevent a recurrence. However, at some point, you may decide that the time used trying to do these repairs is slowing service for homeowners who keep their appointments. In that case, consider using this letter, adapted from *Dear Homeowner:*

> Work order # _____ was issued on _____ for warranty work needed in your home. Several attempts to provide the work listed have been unsuccessful.
>
> After three appointments have been set without obtaining access to a home to provide a repair, our administrative policies and the terms of your warranty provide us with the option to pay you for the work indicated. You can then schedule the needed repair at your convenience and with a repairman of your choice.
>
> A check (#_____) based on the cost to [Builder] for this work is enclosed. The work order will be voided and the item recorded as resolved in your file.
>
> If we can provide you with any information that will assist you in resolving this item on your own, please feel free to call me.

Orientation Items Incomplete or Unacceptable

When a homeowner calls the warranty office—often frustrated or angry—to complain that "Nothing's been done" from the original orientation list, avoid jumping to conclusions. Get the list and go over it with the client, item by item. As you do this, it may turn out that some things are complete and what remains has become annoying to the homeowner, resulting in emotional generalities.

If you can narrow the incomplete items down to a few, communicate immediately with company personnel to get a commitment on when the work will be performed. Follow up with the homeowner to confirm these items are addressed as promised.

If your review of the list with the homeowner indicates that, in fact, "Nothing's been done," set an appointment with the homeowner and ask the individual responsible for getting the work completed to join you. The goal is to create a firm plan for addressing each item and bring all of them to within company standards and to do so quickly. Extra follow up is appropriate in these situations.

Out of Warranty

Service does not stop when the warranty clock strikes 12 months. Many service people find making determinations about out-of-warranty items confusing. Others immediately get defensive and may even be rude to homeowners who have legitimate complaints. This confusion is understandable. Untangle it with the following steps.

- Recognize that out-of-warranty does not automatically mean out of service. Many times the homeowner's request is justified.
- Follow the same steps that apply to warranty requests submitted during the warranty period. Inspect the items and make note of existing conditions.
- Use common sense and look for a fair response. Winning on a technicality means losing clients.
- Understand the circumstances that justify providing repairs after the warranty period has expired; a list of conditions that fit into this category follow.

Grace Period

Grace periods vary from 10 to 30 days past the expiration of warranty. Supposing a homeowner notices a warranty item on the last day of the warranty and that happens to be a Sunday? The grace period provides a common sense time period for a homeowner to notify the builder. Most insured warranty programs include a 30-day grace period.

Code Items

Builders must comply with the codes that applied at the time of construction, regardless of the status of the warranty. These claims often appear when a homeowner sells the home and a hired inspector compiles a report. Warranty insurance policies do not protect builders from code violations.

Contract Items

Builders must fulfill change orders and selection sheets and provide advertised standard features in the home. If the buyer ordered the optional shelves over the laundry and the builder forgot to install them, they must be installed (or the money refunded) even if the homeowner does not notice the omission until the warranty has expired.

Latent Defect

A defect that could not be discovered through normal inspection but was there from the beginning is a latent defect. For example, incorrectly installed valley flashing allowed a slow roof leak. The damage did not appear until the home was 3 years old, and the living room window sills began to rot from the moisture. The flashing was wrong from the beginning but not discernible in a normal inspection. That no one knew it until the warranty expired did not release the builder from repairs under typical implied warranty statutes.

Written Notice

If the homeowner reported an item in writing during the warranty period, but the item was not resolved, the builder must respond even if the warranty has expired. This shows why bringing closure to each item reported, either with a work order, or a documented denial, is important.

Recurring Items

If the same problem was repaired twice or more during the warranty, the failure to repair it satisfactorily might subject the builder to a breach of warranty claim. This concept does not apply to routine repetitive maintenance tasks such as caulking. But if the air conditioner compressor misbehaves the same way it did during the warranty period, the builder's obligation continues.

Manufacturer Covered Claims

Consumer product warranties often provide protection for the homeowner beyond the builder's coverage. The homeowner may require assistance from the builder in these matters, especially since the builder will have more clout with the manufacturer. The builder should provide this assistance not only to help a valued customer, but to learn how well the manufacturer stands behind its products. You may encounter other circumstances that justify repairs outside the warranty period. Remain objective, listen carefully, and investigate fully. When in doubt, err in favor of the homeowner.

Pets

Rarely, but tragically, a homeowner's pet gets loose and is lost or injured during warranty appointments. Less rare is interference in the work by an interested or playful animal. Prevent problems with a caring pet policy, described in your homeowner manual. This example comes from the *Homeowner Manual Template.*

> [Builder] respects the pets that many homeowners count as members of their households. To prevent the possibility of an animal getting injured or lost, or giving in to its natural curiosity about tools and materials used for repairs, we ask that you restrict all animals to a comfortable location during any warranty visit, whether for inspection or warranty work. This policy is also for the protection of our employees and trades personnel. We have instructed [Builder] and trades personnel to reschedule the appointment if pets have access to the work area.

Repetitious Requests

Although your warranty service structure probably provides for one or two standard contacts with homeowners, some homeowners will want more attention. Often the items on repetitious lists are extremely minor, perhaps a reflection of an unusually meticulous personality. They may also be questionable with regard to warranty coverage.

Unless this behavior becomes so common that it causes delays in attention to other homeowners who work within regular checkpoints, simply process the list. If responding begins to impact efficiency, begin with soft approach.

"Mrs. Jones, these are the kind of items we ordinarily address in our 60-day/11-month warranty visit. Would it be okay with you to wait until then?" If the homeowner insists, process the list in the normal manner.

When the situation reaches serious proportions, take a stronger step. Make an appointment to meet with the homeowner, inspect the most recent list, and then sit down to review your normal checkpoints for warranty visits. Take responsibility for the seeming "misunderstanding" about procedures.

"We sometimes fail to call sufficient attention to this information so I'd like to review it with you and explain the reasons for it." A follow-up letter to this meeting might contain wording such as this from *Dear Homeowner*.

> This confirms our conversation of this afternoon. As we discussed, in response to your warranty service requests dated <date>, <date>, <date>, and <date>, I have issued work orders to the appropriate trades.
>
> Your next standard warranty contact will be near the end of your materials and workmanship warranty, during <month>. [Builder] created this system of standard contacts to provide efficient service to all of our homeowners and we appreciate your cooperation with the standard system.
>
> I hope now that I explained the reasons for our system, you will be comfortable working within the standard checkpoints.
>
> Certainly if an emergency occurs you should call us or, outside our business hours, the appropriate trade contractor. If a particular item is causing you great inconvenience, submit a warranty service request. Otherwise our next contact with you will be in <month>.
>
> If you have any questions, please contact me.

However, also be prepared to discover the items this homeowner lists are significant and covered by warranty. When a company delivers a home with an unusual number of real warranty items, extra attention is appropriate. Resist resenting the homeowner for finding and reporting large numbers of items your company did incorrectly. Get them corrected and check on the company systems that produced the problem home.

Requests to Non-Warranty Personnel

We seldom hear of a home buyer coming to the warranty office and asking someone there to prepare a purchase agreement. Yet it is not at all uncommon for homeowners to report warranty items to the sales person or other company personnel with whom they feel an attachment. While this is understandable, the practice does little to produce efficient warranty service.

To address this, train all non-warranty personnel in how to respond. A workable approach is to supply front-line personnel with warranty service request forms. Instruct them to give one to a homeowner who reports warranty items, or even to complete the form on behalf of a homeowner who is upset.

The warranty office also has a responsibility to keep company personnel informed about procedures and volume of work processed. When company personnel have confidence that items reported are addressed promptly and fairly, they feel more comfortable responding to homeowner warranty issues.

Retirees: At Home and Away

Much has been said and written about home design for seniors. Warranty service benefits from adjustments as well. Like all other market segments, these clients share common traits and still have varied desires, values, and housing knowledge. While builders should avoid stereotyping any group of buyers, try to identify frequent behaviors and consider appropriate responses.

What's Your Hurry?

Seniors often operate at a slower pace, physically and in their decision making. This might be due to the freedom from deadlines, work schedules, and the demands of young families. Or this slower pace may come from physical conditions that make moving any faster difficult. Avoid rushing them. This could create doubts, raising the specter of the "fast talking salesman." Likewise, avoid appearing to be annoyed with this slower pace—a message the homeowner may find insulting. Respect the slower pace and plan the time needed for the client to be comfortable.

I'm on a Fixed Income

Even retirees who are financially well-off may be intimidated by knowing that their earning days have ended. Seniors may argue vehemently over even minor items if they feel a maintenance expense is unfair. Your best protection is thorough and early definitions of maintenance responsibilities and warranty commitment.

I'll Die in This House

Thinking this is the last new home they will purchase can add to the pressure for "perfection." While you can understand this, that understanding does little to influence the natural properties of the materials that go into a home. Expect to re-visit such issues several times, whether due to failing memories or faith that persistence will gain the homeowners the attention they want.

New Fangled Gizmos

Unless you have built a home for a member of the senior sub-group that has taken to our world's new technology, correct use of some new home features may elude senior clients. Unable to make the day-night thermostat function, for instance, they may conclude you provided a poor quality product. To prevent this and ensure your homeowners' appreciation and enjoyment of the home, use patience and clear instructions. Then, come back later and offer to answer questions.

Part Time Occupants

Homeowners who prefer specific climates or who left family and friends "back home," may spend part of the year in the new home your company built and part of the year elsewhere. Extended absences pose maintenance concerns, especially where climates are extreme. Consider providing a list of steps homeowners should take to prepare their home before their extended absence. Point out to such clients that the warranty clock continues to tick even if they are in another state (or be prepared to service items reported after the warranty expires).

Full Time Examination

The opposite extreme is just as likely; a retired homeowner who is home all the time may notice hundreds of details, some of which may need attention. If your company sells to this market, expect and plan for extra attention of this type. Clearly identify courtesy items your buyers can expect from your company. Decide ahead of time how many extras you can provide and still keep reasonable control over warranty expenses.

Maintenance Options

Whether for financial or physical reasons, seniors sometimes ask their builder to perform tasks ordinarily thought of as maintenance. If you spend a lot of time working with this market, organizing a pre-priced list of available maintenance items can provide a welcome service to senior homeowners without destroying your warranty service budget. They will appreciate the assistance and your staff will have a positive response when warranty requests include maintenance tasks.

Revenge List

An angry homeowner, disappointed with some aspect of the process or the product, may want to punish the company with long lists of minor items, many of which may be questionable with regard to warranty coverage. Showing no exasperation with this tactic, patiently inspect every item listed, and make appropriate decisions based on reasonable interpretation of your company standards.

At some point in your conversations with this homeowner, you may be faced with an ultimatum. For instance "I have expressed my disappointment with the tree in the front yard several times and have repeatedly been told nothing will be done. If you will replace the tree, I'll forget about these 468 items."

Roof Leaks

Roof leaks are practically guaranteed to make homeowners frantic. This invasion by water conflicts with one of the most fundamental purposes of a home—to protect the occupants from the weather. Homeowners often question the quality of the entire home. One way to mitigate this is a prompt response that includes solid information and rigorous follow-up.

Begin with an empathetic response, making it clear to the homeowner that you take this seriously and intend to correct the problem. Take appropriate actions to contain the damage. Provide a candid explanation and commitment to the homeowner, including the following points:

- Repairs cannot be made while the roof is wet since it is slippery and dangerous.
- The repair order will be given top priority for the next dry day.
- We will not know whether the repair has been successful until mother nature tests the repair several times.
- We will contact you after the next several rains to check on the status of the repair.

This level of attention is easier with a simple reminder system. The format shown in Figure 16.1 works well. Keep it near the warranty phone. After three successful follow-up calls, remove the name from the call list. Even if the leak returns, your homeowners are apt to be more patient because you made a conscientious effort. [Insert Figure 16.1]

Second Owners

If you are contacted by a second (third or fourth) owner with warranty claims, respond courteously and promptly with the following steps:

- Offer to meet with the second homeowners, set an inspection appointment.
- Prior to the appointment, check the warranty file to refresh your memory regarding work. Confirm the status of any pending work orders.
- Review the original orientation list and check for the signature of the first owner confirming these items were completed.
- Pay particular attention to items previously denied and the explanation given.
- Gather copies of appropriate documents to provide to the new homeowners. This would minimally include the applicable homeowner manual.
- Be gracious in your meeting. Introduce yourself, provide a business card and welcome the new homeowners to the community.
- Confirm the new homeowners' phone numbers, and check the spelling of names to update your file.
- Listen to what the new homeowners have to say and inspect items they want to report. Make fair decisions and agree to appropriate repairs if any are needed.
- Explain the repair process, if applicable, and estimate the time frames involved.

Your company has no obligation to provide repairs promised by previous homeowners or any real estate agent involved in the transaction. However, the company should still stand behind its product as it would for the first homeowner.

Some companies state in their limited warranties that coverage terminates upon sale of the home. If serious items are involved, this attitude is unlikely to hold up in a court of law and will certainly not hold up well in the court of public opinion. To homeowners, this position appears to be a ploy used by a builder to sidestep legitimate responsibilities on a contrived technicality.

If you decide that the company has no obligation while the new homeowner insists the first owner or a real estate agent promised repairs would be provided, document your

FIGURE 16.1 Leak Follow Up

Leak Date	Homeowner Phone	Repair Date	Dates of Follow-Up Calls		

answer and suggest that the new homeowner consider contacting the previous homeowner or real estate agent. Take the approach that because they inadvertently created a misunderstanding, they may feel an obligation to participate in making things right.

Signature Negotiations

In a specialized version of "Let's Make a Deal," some homeowners will attempt to bargain for more repairs or items in exchange for their signatures on work orders. Head this power struggle off with information. Consider this homeowner manual entry, which comes from the *Homeowner Manual Template.*

Work Order Signatures
Signing a work order acknowledges that a technician worked in your home on the date shown and with regard to the items listed. It does not negate any of your rights under the warranty nor does it release us from any confirmed warranty obligation. If you prefer not to sign the work order, the technician will note that, sign the work order and return it to us for our records.

Wet Basement

Like roof leaks, another problem that can send homeowners into a frenzy is a wet basement. Uninvited water makes homeowners feel invaded and their belongings, threatened. These problems also share the annoying condition that for a while no one knows whether the problem has been solved. Confidence in a repair increases as time passes and the work is tested.

The homeowners' previous experience has a significant impact on their basement expectations. Being sensitive to this guides your education efforts. Thorough information about the buyer's role in protecting the foundation from water is vital and should be included in your homeowner manual.

When a wet basement report comes in, respond promptly. While builder definitions of emergency seldom include "uninvited water in basement," many homeowners feel the term exactly describes their situation.

If more than dampness or a minor amount of water is reported, or if the homeowner is highly emotional about the occurrence, inspect the home as soon as possible. For the inspection, a sheet such as the one shown in Figure 16.2 acts as a guide to investigate and document conditions. Having a clear procedure reassures the homeowners that someone who knows what to do is taking charge. This increases the homeowner's confidence in your actions or advice.

If builder error caused the problem, prompt repairs are essential along with follow up over several months to confirm the solution worked. If homeowner actions are the cause, suggest appropriate corrections and then offer to inspect those corrections when the homeowner has made them. Take a friendly approach rather than a scolding one. Document your recommendations in a follow-up letter.

FIGURE 16.2 Wet Basement

Homeowner _____ Lot# _____

Address _____ Floor Plan _____

_____ Closing Date _____

Phone (H) _____ Inspection Date _____

Phone (W) _____ By _____

House File   **Notes**

☐ Grade plan
☐ Final survey
☐ Quality management inspections
☐ Orientation list
☐ Warranty document and guidelines
☐ Previous warranty requests
☐ Previous inspection reports
☐ Phone logs
☐ Correspondence

Existing Grade and Landscaping

☐ Photos
☐ Slope at foundation
☐ Landscape materials in backfill area
☐ Edging
☐ Downspout extension/splashblocks?
☐ Location of trees or large shrubs
☐ Sprinkler system
☐ Water service
☐ Drainage from neighboring lots
☐ Homeowner additions

Interior Conditions

☐ Foundation cracks
☐ Floor cracks
☐ Crawl space condition
☐ Penetrations (form ties, utility lines)
☐ First entry location
☐ Area affected
☐ Perimeter drain
☐ Sump pit
☐ Sump pump
☐ Water lines
☐ Sewer lines
☐ Condensation
☐ Homeowner B/M construction?

Conclusion

Anonymous once said "If you can keep your head when those around you are losing theirs, you probably don't understand the situation."

Achieving client satisfaction requires that you understand the situation and keep your head— check on details, make fair decisions, follow through on commitments, document every occurrence, hold your temper, manage your mouth, and smile as you do all of the above (and more). Anyone who thinks these tasks are simple or easy has not tried to do them.

The challenges are richly varied, a good portion created by your own company and more coming from clients. Many courageous individuals, with grace and skill, step up to these challenges, meet them, and succeed, then go home with inadequate compensation— financial and emotionally

You may question your resolve and your sanity. Let me assure you–

- Your efforts, while endless, are worthy. Be resilient.
- Your knowledge, while growing, stops before the questions do. Keep learning.
- Your frustrations, while justified, can seem futile. Give objective data to those who can make changes.
- Your paper trail, while voluminous, is seldom complete. Keep documenting.
- Your trades, while heroic, can also be goats. Thank one as you nag another.
- Your company's reputation, while perhaps imperfect, is better thanks to your work.
- Your commitment, while burning out, is among the strongest in the industry.

Why do you do all this?

Clearly, you are nuts.

By the way, your phone is ringing.

Resources

The products listed below can help you with your work in meeting with clients by providing additional information for you or the client. They were published by BuilderBooks, National Association of Home Builders, in Washington, D.C. For additional information about these products, go to www.BuilderBooks.com or call 800-223-2665.

Books

Gerhart, James. *Caring for your Home. A guide to maintaining Your Investment.* Washington, 2005. 150 pp.

Jaffe, David. *Contracts and Liability,* 5th ed. 2004. 214 pp.

Smith, Carol. *Building Your Home: An insider's Guide,* 2nd ed. 2005. 177 pp.

_____. Customer Service for home Builders, 2003. 116 pp.

_____. *Dear Homeowner: A book of Customer Service Letters.* 2001. 160 pp. With CD.

_____. *Homeowner Manual: A Template for home Builders,* 2nd e. 2001. 225 pp. With disk.

_____. *Warranty Service for home Builders.* 2003, 116 pp.

Booklets

Building Your New Home. 2001. 52 pp.

Buying Your New Home. 2003. 30 pp.

Your New home and how to Take Care of It. 2003. 64 pp.